Streets of Bloomsbury & Fitzrovia

D1004193

ISBN 0 904491 38 2

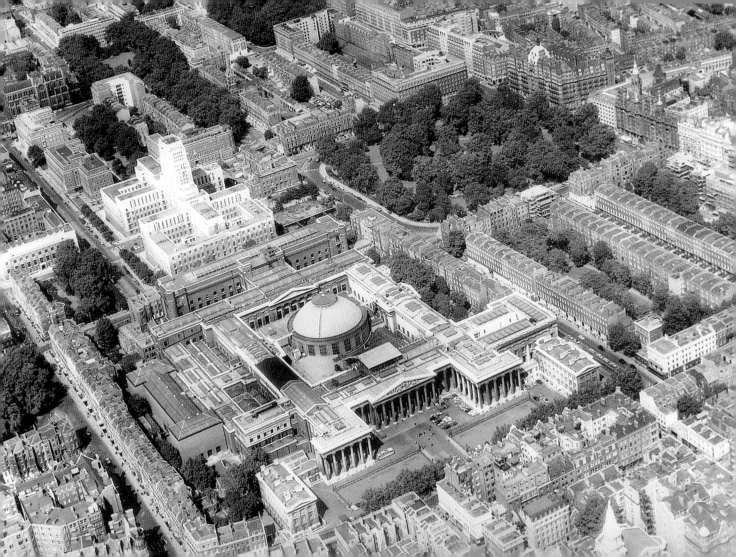

Streets of Bloomsbury & Fitzrovia

A survey of streets, buildings & former residents in a part of Camden

Compiled by	Camden History Society's Research Team
Edited by	F Peter Woodford
Designed by	Ivor Kamlish

Map 1. Diagrammatic map of the area described, with section numbers

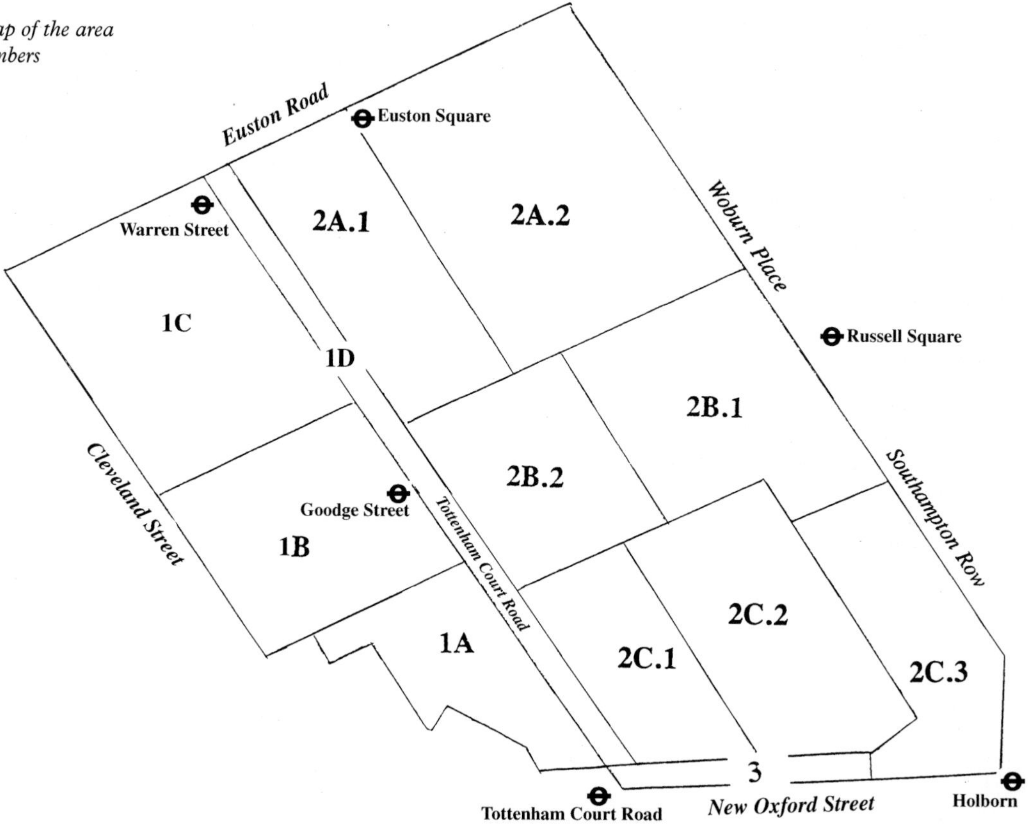

Euston Road

Euston Square

Warren Street

2A.1

2A.2

Woburn Place

1C

1D

Russell Square

Cleveland Street

2B.1

2B.2

Goodge Street

Tottenham Court Road

Southampton Row

1B

1A

2C.2

2C.1

2C.3

3

Tottenham Court Road

New Oxford Street

Holborn

Contents

THIS BOOK covers some of the grandest architecture in the Borough of Camden, dealing as it does with the purlieus of the Bedford Estate in Bloomsbury, on which some of the best houses from the best period of domestic architecture in Britain were built, and which are still to be seen and admired. There are fine Adam houses in Fitzroy Square too, and other 18th-century houses scattered about the rest of Fitzrovia. But the interest of these two areas does not lie only in architectural grandeur: these streets have been home to a multitude of great artists, writers, lawyers and doctors clustering round the British Museum, University College and its hospitals (now including the Middlesex) and the Senate House of London University. Not to mention the notorious 'Bloomsbury Group' or Set, centred on Fitzroy and Gordon Squares.

We describe the streets - and what we can deduce of their history from a wide variety of sources listed on p 91 - in a series of walkable itineraries, each of which starts from a stop on the Tube or bus lines which surround or penetrate the areas. Much can be seen in the state in which it was erected, though much too has been destroyed by bombing or redevelopment. We hope we have been able to re-create, or at least hint at, the atmosphere of former times while celebrating the beauty of what remains and has been lovingly preserved.

**The Bloomsbury & Fitzrovia
Research Team**

Sheila Ayres	David Hellings
Steve Denford	Tatiana Wolff
Liz Eccleshare	Peter Woodford
David Hayes	Robin Woolven

April 1997

Illustrations

The following courteously provided and gave permission to reproduce illustrations: David Hayes (maps); Aerofilms Ltd, Architectural Review, Camden Local Studies and Archive Centre, Country Life, Horizon, Illustrated London News, National Monuments Record, National Portrait Gallery, Sir John Soane's Museum, the Society of Friends.

Historical overview to about 1830

(see maps on pp 10-11)

By the late 17th century, London had broken out of the confines of its ancient wall: from the street connecting the City with Westminster, a continuous built-up area now stretched northwards to Holborn, reaching as far as the ancient church of **St Giles-in-the-Fields**. However, the northern half of its parish, with which much of this book is concerned, was still rural. There was a large Liquorice Field growing medicinal plants between what are now Bury Place and Coptic Street, and a cherry orchard covered what is now Bloomsbury Square. Most of the fields served as pasture for dairy cattle.

Much of our area lay in the manor of Bloomsbury, earlier known as **Blemundsbury**, after William de Blemund, who in 1201 bought land here previously granted to the Abbey of Westminster by Edward the Confessor. To drain the then marshy ground he made a ditch, known as Blemund's Dyke, along the present line of Bloomsbury Way and Vernon Place. William Blémont or Blemund was the brother of an Anglo-Norman merchant either with a mansion near Cornhill, or married to an heiress

called Cornhill (accounts differ), adopting the name Blémont as a gallicised version of Cornhill. The estate acquired and retained the name Blemundsbury even though it only remained in the family for three generations. It subsequently passed through many hands until its owner in 1375, a wealthy fishmonger called Nicholas Exton, made a deal with the monks of the London Charterhouse by which he bequeathed the manor to them in return for a life annuity for himself and his family.

At the Dissolution, Henry VIII annexed all the estates of the Charterhouse and in 1545 gave 'the messuage called Blumsbery and the fields northwards' to his Lord Chancellor, Thomas Wriothesley, later created Earl of **Southampton**. Between 1201 and 1545 someone had built a twin-gabled manor house at the south-east corner of the property, just south of Blemund's Dyke (Vernon Place), which its new owners renamed Southampton House.

The earls of Southampton farmed the estate throughout the Tudor period and through the reigns of three Stuarts. The 3rd earl was allowed by James I to extend his estate southwards from Blemund's Dyke to High Holborn over what had previously been the 'king's gore', gaining a valuable increase in frontage to that road to the west. The Southampton title was extinguished when in 1667 the 4th earl died without male issue. Rachel, his

daughter and co-heiress, and the widow of Lord Vaughan, married William Russell, eldest son of the 5th earl (later, 1st duke) of **Bedford**. Lord William was executed for treason in 1683, but the manor passed to his son, and much of what we shall be describing is still part of the Bedford estate.

The remainder of our area lay in the manor of **Tottenhall**, part of **St Pancras**, a large parish stretching some 4 miles north to Highgate. The Tottenhall manor house, known as **Tottenham Court**, once stood just outside our area between what are now Euston Road and Tolmers Square. The Domesday Book (1086) recorded the manor as belonging to the Canons of St Paul's Cathedral. It was confiscated by Parliament in the 1640s, and given to one Ralph Harrison, but reclaimed by the Crown at the Restoration (1660). Seven years later it was leased to Henry Benet, Earl of Arlington, of Euston Hall, Suffolk. His daughter Isabella married Henry **Fitzroy**, an illegitimate son of Charles II, who became Earl of **Euston** and Duke of **Grafton**. Charles Fitzroy, the second son of the 2nd duke, who inherited the family's Tottenhall property in 1757, later became the 1st **Baron Southampton** - a new creation, independent of the title which had become extinct over a century earlier. Thus, by historical accident, we have within our area two adjoining properties, both known at different times as the Southampton estate, though they belonged to two unrelated families.

Between the two ducal estates, on either side of Tottenham Court Lane (now Road), were several smaller holdings. Among these were the **City Lands**, owned by the City Corporation since 1441, and located in the vicinity of present-day Alfred Place (p 66).

During the Civil War, fortifications were constructed against a possible attack on London by Royalist forces based in Oxford. Earthen bulwarks lined what was then the northern edge of London, passing some way north of Southampton House. Forts were built in its fields, and to the west of Tottenham Court Lane in Crab Tree Field (Map 2). The earthworks, never tested in battle, were not dismantled till long after the War: those in Bloomsbury were incorporated into the gardens of the great houses soon to be erected there.

The earl of Southampton had wanted to build himself a modern house since before the Civil War, but royal policy forbade the erection of important London houses beyond the City walls, and he obtained permission to do so only at the Restoration. Emulating the Russells' development 30 years earlier in Covent Garden, the 4th earl laid out Southampton (now Bloomsbury) Square, with his new house (later Bedford House) on its north side and a 'little town' to the south to service it, complete with shops and market.

A neighbouring plot was offered to the Duke of Montagu, an in-law of the Wriothesleys, on which to build (1678) Montagu House, the second version of which, after a fire destroyed the first, later became the first home of the British Museum.

Plague and fire (1665-66) prompted further westward migration from the City. Houses were built in the 1680s on the Pitaunce Croft immediately north of St Giles church. These would eventually degenerate into the notorious slums of the Rookery, which were finally swept away in the mid-1840s by the building of New Oxford Street - our southern boundary, and the subject of Section 3. By 1720 the whole area from Great Russell Street southwards was built up. In the 1720s the first houses of North Soho (now known as Fitzrovia) had been built, see section 1A. 1731 saw the creation of a new parish, St George's Bloomsbury, carved out of the parish of St Giles and corresponding, very roughly, to Bloomsbury manor.

The fields to the north remained as farmland. Agricultural needs often conflicted with those of the townsfolk, who would come here to walk, gather watercress, shoot ducks, or indulge in rough games. The redoubtable dairy-farming Capper sisters (Bedford tenants) are said to have patrolled their fields on horseback, confiscating the clothes of boys found bathing illicitly in one of the many ponds

which dotted the area, and cutting the strings of any kite-flying youngsters with a pair of shears carried for the purpose.

The northward march of the built-up area resumed in the second half of the 18th century, encouraged by the building of the world's first urban by-pass, the **New Road** from Paddington to Islington. Authorised by Act of Parliament in 1756, it was meant to ease the movement of troops and to enable cattle to be driven to the City markets while avoiding the congested streets of Holborn and St Giles. Renamed Euston Road in 1857, its Camden section, now much widened, forms the northern boundary for our area. In the controversy surrounding the road's construction, Grafton and Bedford, our ducal neighbours, were in opposing camps. Grafton, an active supporter, saw the road as an opportunity. In 1768 he shrewdly purchased the freehold of the Tottenhall demesne lands from St Paul's at a bargain price, securing development rights over some 255 acres, including the Home Field and Murrells, sites respectively of Fitzroy and Euston Squares. The 4th duke of Bedford opposed the by-pass, fearing the loss of his fine views northward to Hampstead and Highgate. The road was built, and the inevitable urbanisation of the fields to its south was soon under way.

West of Tottenham Court Lane, land ownership was fragmented, development haphazard and piecemeal. Fields were

*Map 2. Diagrammatic representation
of the major original estates underlying present
Bloomsbury and Fitzrovia.*

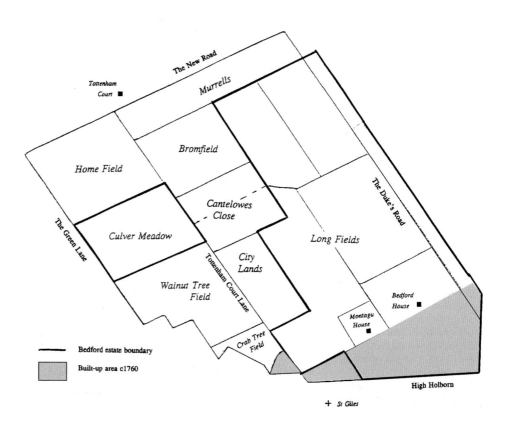

The New Road

Tottenham
Court ■

Murrells

Bromfield

Home Field

The Green Lane

Culver Meadow

*Cantelowes
Close*

The Duke's Road

Long Fields

Tottenham Court Lane

*City
Lands*

*Walnut Tree
Field*

*Bedford
House* ■

*Montagu
House* ■

*Crab Tree
Field*

———— Bedford estate boundary

Built-up area c1760

High Holborn

✠ *St Giles*

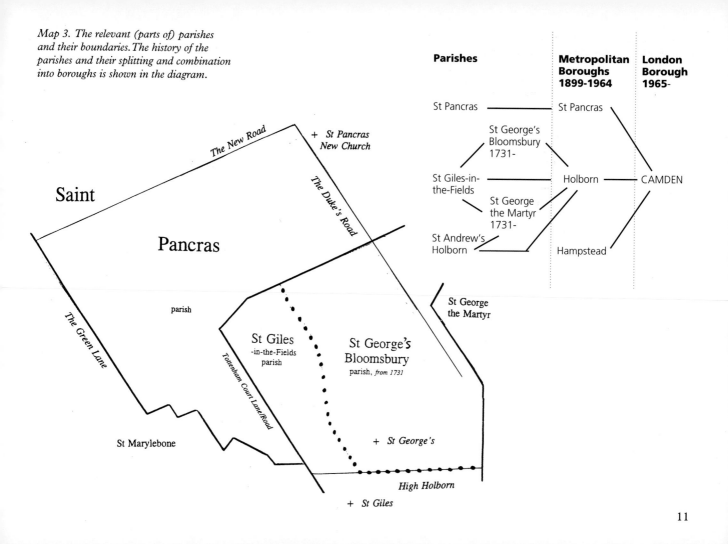

Map 3. The relevant (parts of) parishes and their boundaries. The history of the parishes and their splitting and combination into boroughs is shown in the diagram.

Parishes

Metropolitan Boroughs 1899-1964

London Borough 1965-

St Pancras — St Pancras

St George's Bloomsbury 1731-

St Giles-in-the-Fields — Holborn — CAMDEN

St George the Martyr 1731-

St Andrew's Holborn

Hampstead

+ St Pancras New Church

Saint

Pancras

The New Road

The Duke's Road

The Green Lane

parish

Tottenham Court Lane/Road

St Giles -in-the-Fields parish

St George's Bloomsbury parish, from 1731

St George the Martyr

St Marylebone

+ St George's

High Holborn

+ St Giles

developed one by one, ever northwards, as their owners leased plots to numerous small speculative builders, and by the 1770s houses covered Walnut Tree Field as far north as Chitty Street. With no single influential landlord to enforce standards, North Soho evolved into a crowded, cosmopolitan, but generally poor area of formerly grand houses degraded by multiple occupancy, cheaper dwellings, retail premises and workshops, many of the latter serving the furniture industry.

On the ducal estates, development was just as fitful, but here it was planned, and entrusted to architects or speculative builders of stature. Wide streets and grand squares fit for the gentry were the order of the day - though in fact the cream of society had migrated further west to Mayfair, Hyde Park and Belgravia.

On the Bedford estate, the 4th duke apparently repented of his opposition to the New Road; to improve access to it he upgraded an old track along his eastern boundary (on the line of Woburn Place) into a private road. A Bedford Circus projected in the 4th duke's time materialised after his death in 1771 as Bedford Square. His widow was a driving force behind the onward development of the estate: she began the lower end of Gower Street, bought land in Cantelowes Close from the Duke of Newcastle to lay out what is now Torrington Place, and developed Culver Meadow (west of

Tottenham Court Road). In the same spirit the 5th duke, her grandson, gave up his 1660 town house (Bedford House) in 1800 and commissioned James Burton, John Nash's favourite builder, to demolish it and develop the land northwards. Burton built Bedford Place, Russell Square and the east side of Tavistock Square.

After a hiatus during the Napoleonic Wars, Tavistock Square was completed in 1820 by Thomas Cubitt, the first builder to employ a permanent skilled workforce. He started work on Gordon Square in the 1820s, but financial difficulties delayed its completion, by his executors, until 40 years later. Torrington and Woburn Squares were built by James Sim and his family in 1821-28, but a projected Carmarthen Square was pre-empted by the building of University College (UCL).

Meanwhile, Lord Southampton had laid out Fitzroy Square on his Home Field, two sides of it designed by no less than the Adam brothers. Begun in 1792, and intended as the centrepiece of a self-contained suburb with a market, the square was finished only in 1835. By this time Euston Square had arisen to the east astride the Euston Road; this is the only one of the squares laid out in the 18th and 19th centuries that has been eliminated by subsequent development (see p 50).

Thus, gradually and in different ways, Bloomsbury and Fitzrovia grew up side by side. By about 1830 the development of

our area was all but complete, and a street pattern substantially unchanged to this day was in place. The steady expansion of UCL and the University of London, inevitable decays in the fabric with time, the devastations of two World Wars and the march of commercial development described in later pages have wrought many changes, but many of the original buildings and layouts can still be admired, and there is much of interest in what is new. The history of this most attractive part of central London is replete with colourful stories of its distinguished and its disreputable inhabitants.

The 'Bloomsbury Group'

The term 'Bloomsbury Group' (sometimes, 'Set') is applied to a group of intellectuals, artists, writers and others living in the area and in close intellectual contact, active during the first two decades of the 20th century. It is not our purpose to assess the achievements or to detail all its members, merely to mention leading players and their associations with the area, as background to the specific mentions made elsewhere in this book. The centre of gravity of the Group in fact was at different times as much in Fitzrovia as in Bloomsbury.

What was later recognised as the Bloomsbury Group originally formed around the former Cambridge University friends of Thoby Stephen (1880-1906), the brother of Vanessa (1879-1961) and Virginia Stephen (1881-1941). Virginia's education was fragmentary because of her poor health and was largely based on the library of her father Sir Leslie Stephen (1832-1904), eminent Victorian man of letters and the first editor (1882-1891) of the *Dictionary of National Biography*, where (according to his successor and memorialist) he rejected entries he found guilty of sentimental eulogy, demanding unembroidered fact. Lady Stephen (who was Julia Prinsep, widow of Herbert Duckworth, the publisher) died in 1895 and Sir Leslie in 1904, when Virginia had the first of her nervous breakdowns. The sisters and younger brother Adrian (1883-1948) then moved from Hyde Park Gate into Bloomsbury, taking a lease on **46 Gordon Square** late in 1904.

In 1905 Vanessa continued the tradition of 'at homes' set by Thoby by starting a weekly 'Friday Group' of meetings of artists and intellectuals. When Vanessa married Clive Bell in 1907, Virginia and Adrian moved out to **29 Fitzroy Square** where Virginia ran her own evening 'Thursday Group', whose members often overlapped with Vanessa's Friday Group. Thoby's death from typhoid fever in 1906 had caused Virginia to suffer a prolonged period of depression and nervous instability but, when in town, she kept up her Thursday evening activities at Fitzroy Square.

Other leading members in the Bloomsbury Group (a term they did not themselves use) included the biographer Lytton Strachey (1880-1932), the economist John Maynard (later Lord) Keynes (1883-1946), the art critics Roger Fry (1866-1934) and Clive Bell (1881-1964), Leonard Woolf (1880-1969), Civil Servant Saxon Sydney-Turner, Walter (later Sir Walter) Lamb, long-serving Secretary of the Royal Academy, and author and critic Desmond MacCarthy (1878-1952). In 1909, while a Fellow at King's College Cambridge, J M Keynes shared rooms at 21 Fitzroy Square with the artist Duncan Grant (1885-1978), a member of the London Group and, like Vanessa Bell, well represented in the Tate Gallery. When in 1916 Vanessa moved to Sussex with Duncan Grant, Keynes moved into 46 Gordon Square, which the Bells had vacated, and lived there till his death in 1946.

The Bloomsbury Group mixed a rich and refined culture with a declared opposition to the religious and moral standards of Victorian orthodoxy, and lived up to their own standards with distinctly unorthodox behaviour.

In 1911 Virginia Stephen, by then a noted literary critic, moved from Fitzroy Square to share a house at 38 Brunswick Square with Leonard Woolf and others. Virginia married Leonard in 1912 and moved to Richmond. After another serious breakdown occasioned by the outbreak of World War I, she started writing her highly original novels. In 1917 her husband set up the Hogarth Press as a therapeutic interest for Virginia, first at Hogarth House, Paradise Road, Richmond and later (1924) in the basement of the house to which they had moved, back in their beloved Bloomsbury, **52 Tavistock Square**. The Press subsequently published all of Virginia's books, with dust jackets designed by Vanessa. The couple also had a country house at Rodmell, in Sussex. They moved from Tavistock Square to 37 Mecklenburgh Square in 1939 which, like their former house in Tavistock Square, was also bombed out in September 1940.

Roger Fry organised the pioneering Post-Impressionist exhibitions in London's Grafton Gallery in 1910 and 1912. For the second exhibition the catalogue noted that "prices of pictures may be obtained on application to Mr Leonard Woolf, who will attend the Galleries in the afternoons"; the English pictures were selected by Clive Bell, and the executive committee (secretary, Desmond MacCarthy) included Lady Ottoline Morrell (1837-1938, p 65), herself a centre of literary and art circles in London. In July 1913 Roger Fry opened his Omega Workshops Ltd at **33 Fitzroy Square** "for the production of well-designed articles of daily use" (p 32) in collaboration with Duncan Grant and Clive and Vanessa Bell. Many artists were involved in the Omega Workshops, which Percy Wyndham Lewis left in 1915 after a disagreement - then setting up the Vorticist movement.

It would be tedious to trace all the links and associations of the Bloomsbury Group, but mention must be made of the contemporary artists living and working in the Fitzroy Street area, such as Walter Sickert, Harold Gilman and Augustus John - variously members of the Camden Town Group, the Euston Road Group, the London Group and the New English Art Club. All were peripherally associated with the Bloomsbury Group which, by any standards, was undoubtedly the most important intellectual grouping of the period, however much mocked by those not admitted or those who failed to stay the course once introduced.

1: Fitzrovia
Introduction

In 1940 William Hickey in the *Daily Express* described the bohemian set that met at the Fitzroy Tavern as Fitzrovians. The name quickly became associated with the whole area, once referred to as North Soho, which lies between Oxford Street and Euston Road. The area has, for much of its history, been somewhat down-at-heel but at the same time intellectual and/or artistic (Fig 1).

Its first street, Rathbone Place, was in the 1720s distinctly aristocratic, the impetus for its development being the successful Cavendish estate, also to the north of Oxford Street but further west. In Fitzrovia, mainly developed after 1760, most houses were of good quality. But the relentless move of fashion westward meant that houses increasingly became divided and sublet. Rents were low but rooms were large: excellent for studios. Fitzrovia has always attracted a literary and artistic community: before 1800 two-thirds of all newly appointed members of the Royal Academy took houses in the district, especially in Charlotte Street, where they were surrounded by others involved in the art trade, some of whom remained to supply more impoverished artists in the 19th century. Then, shop fronts were added and small craft workshops appeared.

A little before 1900 foreign immigrants moved in, increasing the variety of small specialist businesses and restaurants with which the area abounds. At that time it acquired a reputation for anarchy and insurrection, with Communist and anarchist clubs. In the early 20th century many writers and again artists, some of them members of the Bloomsbury Group, lived and worked locally.

Parts of Fitzrovia, particularly Whitfield Street, were badly damaged during World War II; parts also suffered at the hands of planners and developers. While their wilder dreams did not materialise, many terraces have been replaced by multi-storey office blocks or student halls, especially north of Howland Street, which is now dominated by the 620-foot Telecom Tower. An influx of media, advertising and architectural businesses has, however, moderated the rate and style of change. Streets once seedy have been repaired and several buildings around Fitzroy Square are now listed.

A recognised community of some 5000 permanent residents has its own Neighbourhood Association organising an annual festival, and its own local newspaper, the *Fitzrovia Neighbourhood News*, founded in 1980. A recent innovation is the Fitzrovia Partnership which involves businesses, the two boroughs (Westminster and Camden) in which it lies, voluntary organisations and residents.

The east-west limits of Fitzrovia are often set at Gower Street and Great Portland Street, but we shall concentrate on the area formerly in St Pancras - west of Tottenham Court Road and east of Cleveland Street. Our walks, zigzagging through the area from Tottenham Court Road Underground station to Warren Street Underground station, thus lie mainly in the borough of Camden, although at the start we will trespass into Westminster. A second walk (route 1D) takes us straight down the Tottenham Court Road from north to south.

16

Tottenham Court Road station to Goodge Street through southern Fitzrovia

Take Exit 2, Oxford Street (North), from Tottenham Court Road Underground station and emerge on the west side of **TOTTENHAM COURT ROAD**. This busy one-way street is now probably best known for the electronics shops at its southern end, but the main outlets of the furniture trade which characterised it earlier remain at its northern end. It has always been one of London's major thoroughfares leading north to Hampstead: a market road led from St Giles through the fields of Tottenhall Manor, or Tottenham Court as it became known after 1600. Section 1D (p 34) takes us on a walk down Tottenham Court Road from its northern extremity by Warren Street station to where we are now; for the moment we shall walk north up it a short distance and then plunge westwards into Fitzrovia.

Just to our right, the St Giles Pound stood from 1656 until 1765, and there was a large circular parish boundary stone set

1 Osbert Lancaster's 1942 cartoon of Fitzrovia: not accurate, but captures the atmosphere of the time.

in the middle of the road at which, according to J T Smith, Charity boys beating the bounds might themselves be beaten. Roughly where we are standing there was until 1900 an isolated row of

---

Street names along route 1A and their origin

Charlotte
George III's queen
Evelyn
land-owning family
Goodge
land-owning family
Gresse
Peter Gresse bought this land in 1752
Hanway
John Hanway bought this land in 1705
Percy
family name of dukes of Northumberland
Rathbone
Thomas Rathbone inherited a house here
Stephen
Stephen Lemaistre, neighbour of Gresse
Tottenham Court
originally Tottenhall Manor, was brought (along with Euston, Suffolk) to Henry Fitzroy, Duke of Grafton, by marriage
Windmill
a 16th-century windmill was here

---

tall old houses known as Boziers Court (popularly called Boozers Court, from its corner pub) impeding the flow of traffic.

The striped brick building to our left was a large clothing store (as it is now) erected in 1893 in the shadow of Boziers Court just before the Court was demolished.

A few yards farther on, Virgin's Megastore on the left occupies the site of the Oxford Music Hall, which opened in 1861 (on the site of the galleried yard of the Boar and Castle Inn) and staged the first performance of the can-can in England. It was rebuilt twice: on opening night in 1892 Marie Lloyd topped the bill with "Oh, Mr Porter". It was pulled down in 1926 and replaced by a Lyons Corner House whose ornate façade is still visible.

By the side of the **Blue Posts** pub, here since at least 1770, but single-storeyed now after WW II bombing, we leave the bustle of Tottenham Court Road and turn left for the calm of **HANWAY STREET**. The southern boundary of Tottenhall manor was just short of Oxford Street, leaving a small meadow mainly in St Marylebone (note the parish boundary marker on **No.14**). This land was bought in 1705 by retired Major John Hanway (1672-1736), the uncle of the philanthropist Jonas Hanway who in the face of much derision popularised the use of the umbrella. Hanway Street is first mentioned in an Overseer's survey in 1723 when 14 houses are listed, including one shop. In the 18th century it formed the main route, avoiding the unsavoury St Giles Pound, from Oxford Street to Bloomsbury, and from 1805 to 1807 the philosopher William Godwin, Shelley's father-in-law, had a bookshop here under his *nom-de-plume* Edward Baldwin. The street was known for its lace, milliners and toy shops into the Victorian period, and later for china and curiosity shops. Now, there are several cafés alongside specialist shops for collectors of old rock, pop and jazz records.

Passing Hanway Place we reach **No.18** ('Vinyl Experience'), a red-brick 1720s town house topped by two stone finials of flaming urns. Next door, **No.20**, also old, is covered in a mural featuring Blue Meanies from the Beatles' cartoon film, *The Yellow Submarine*. Most of the south side to our left is taken up by the articulated wall of what was before the first World War Frascati's restaurant and winter gardens (now the Costa Dorada).

The road gets even narrower as it winds its way into Oxford Street. On No.46 to our left a plaque records that the street was widened 6 feet here in 1841.

Turn right into Oxford Street and right again into **RATHBONE PLACE**, named after Captain Thomas Rathbone (died 1721) whose family had had a house here since the 1680s. Note the plaque on the side of the bank on the corner, "Rathbone Place in Oxford Street 1718". The street was first mentioned in an Overseer's survey in 1723 when there were 29 houses of some distinction, most commanding

annual rents of £30. Until the 1760s Rathbone Place terminated at Marchant's waterworks with its large pond and windmill. This provided auxiliary power to the pump in Hartshorn Lane (near Charing Cross) which was driven by the flow of sewage (Marchant's water was never very popular!). The offices of the company were in Rathbone Place.

The street was still respectable in the late 18th century, but it was then taken over by commercial users, and by 1817 only one private house remained. A few old houses stand at the north end, but the west side has almost completely given way to the architectural disaster (1960s) of the Royal Mail Sorting Office.

On this side, however, **Nos.51-52** still houses Winsor and Newton, artists' colourmen, first established at No.38 in 1832 before expansion. Opposite is the **Black Horse** in a mid-19th-century stock brick building, with a cornice and very grand lamps. The pub was here from at least 1746, when what is now **EVELYN YARD** (renamed in 1937 after the Evelyn family, owners of the land in 1767) was called Black Horse Yard. This gated yard, into which we now turn, used to contain a number of stores and small factories, but these were all bombed in WW II and it now serves as a car park. If we bear left across it we can reach

GRESSE STREET, where nothing remains to show that this was one of the

earliest streets in the area. We are now in what were once the Crabtree and Walnut Tree Fields, which stretched from here (just north of Hanway's land) as far as present-day Chitty Street. The main part was leased by the Goodge family but the southern part, as far as Percy Street, was leased in 1717 by John Hassell, a brewer, who soon afterwards built some houses there. On the rest of the land he had a house and garden. His estate was bought in 1752 by Peter Gaspard Gresse (the Swiss father of the painter Alexander John Gresse, later drawing master to the children of George III, who called him Mr Grease because of his bulk). Gresse completed the street in 1767, and in collaboration with his neighbour Stephen Lemaistre laid out **Stephen Street** (the turning now leading under Metropolis House to Tottenham Court Road), on the site of Hassell's house and garden in 1768. An auction of the early 1780s talks of "substantial brick dwellings in an airy part of town", not an impression gained today.

The blocks which loom above us across the road were part of the bitterly contested EMI development of the 1970s which swept away many old houses in Stephen Street as well as the numerous small workshops of Tudor Place once directly ahead of us. The curving block on our left at **Nos.7-15 Gresse Street** is an annexe of Birkbeck College, whose main building is in Malet Street (p 61).

Past Birkbeck College Gresse Street turns left and we reach Rathbone Place again. Turn right and pass the mock-Tudor **Wheatsheaf** pub, in the 1930s the haunt of writers such as Dylan Thomas who had decamped from the Fitzroy Tavern when it became too well known. Thomas is said to have been introduced to his future wife, Caitlin McNamara, by Augustus John here in 1936. At this northern end there is a handful of old houses. No.27 is on the site of the house in which the Rev Henry and Mrs Matthews lived from 1766 to 1804. He was the vicar of nearby Percy Chapel (said to have been built for him) and a patron of Flaxman, who sculpted small figures for niches in their back room, where Mrs Matthews held her regular *conversazioni*. These allowed writers and poets to reach a wide and discerning audience. J T Smith, in his *Book For A Rainy Day*, said here he heard William Blake read (and sing!) his poems, which the Matthewses helped Blake to publish. Fern and Co. moved here from Newman Street in 1903, and the impressive solid mahogany fittings in the shop date from then. The firm supplies much of the coffee that is drunk in nearby restaurants.

Across the street, note the houses north of the sorting office. **No.33** is where John Harris Heal, founder of Heal's, set up a bed-making and furniture business in 1810 before moving in 1818 to 203 Tottenham Court Road. **Nos.31** and 30 are four-storeyed 18th-century buildings with brick parapets. In **No.30**, now stuccoed and with an early shop front, Nathaniel Hone RA (1718- 84) lived from 1780 until his death. He was best known for his painting The Conjuror, which satirised Joshua Reynolds' penchant for borrowing from the Old Masters. When it was rejected by the Academy he set up the first independent exhibition organised by an artist. In the early 19th century this house was part of the adjoining Percy Hotel & Coffee House at **No.29**, mentioned in 1768 by James Boswell. The hotel closed during the 1840s. A parish boundary plate can be seen on the wall.

At the corner of Rathbone Place and Percy Street, look north along **CHARLOTTE STREET**. This was begun in the early 1760s, soon after George III came to the throne, and originally extended from Percy Street to Goodge Street. By 1764 the east side was complete, with elegant five-storey houses roofed with blue slate. On the west side, on the site of the windmill, a chapel of ease was built 1764-5 by William Franks. This 'Percy Chapel' opened on 5 January 1766, the Rev Henry Matthews being its minister till 1804. Wilberforce worshipped here. The chapel was demolished in 1867.

Charlotte Street was the artists' centre in the 18th century, when several members of the Royal Academy lived here. Giles Walkley has written that a spell in Charlotte Street or neighbouring streets was essential for aspiring artists. Not only were cheap rooms to be had and easily altered, but comradeship, expert advice, models, drawing schools, colourmen and frame-makers were all available. Engravers lived here too. Wealthy painters built on rooms for studios, while others made do with 'cut-up' windows (windows extended upwards) in former parlours.

As leases fell in during the 19th century the houses were not demolished but, as Summerson has written, "swathed in compo detail". This can be seen at **No.2** diagonally opposite, now one of the many restaurants and pavement cafés at this southern end of Charlotte Street. The building has Ionic stucco pilasters along its side wall in **PERCY STREET**, down which we now walk. This romantic tree-lined street was developed between 1764 and 1767.

Despite war damage, refacing and internal alteration, Percy Street remains a street of fine 18th-century houses. Indeed, it was one of the first realisations of the urban Classical ideal: a uniform and classically composed street. Doors in the centre houses probably had pedimented and Ionic columned porches (as at Nos.12 and 30), while other houses had corniced or consoled surrounds (as at Nos.9, 13, 19, 20, 28, 32 and 33). End houses also broke forward to form pavilions.

On the south side **No.1**, The White Tower, was originally a restaurant and hotel called *La Tour Eiffel*. In 1914 the Vorticists Percy Wyndham Lewis and Ezra Pound met here to celebrate the launch of their magazine BLAST. Lewis painted a wall of one of the upper rooms, but the painting has gone. In the 1920s the circle of Augustus John and Nina Hamnett regularly wined and dined here before they deserted the restaurant for the more down-to-earth Fitzroy Tavern. **No.4** is faced in very attractive Art Nouveau terracotta tiles, with detailing in green and yellow, right up to the cornice. Wyndham Lewis had rooms here in 1914. Since 1962 it has housed Beardmore's brass foundry firm, founded 1860 in Cleveland Street. Their motto is "anything from a tin-tack to a dreadnought" (a dreadnought is in fact a file). Next door at **No.5** William Franks, the builder responsible for much of the development of the Goodge Estate, lived from 1770 until 1788, two years before his death.

Across the street **Nos.34-37** (Grade II listed) have simple moulded arched doorways and **No.33** has an early shop front. Passing Nos.7 and 8 on this side, note the 'cut-up' windows at first-floor level denoting artists' studios. At **No.8**, the miniaturist Francis Samuel Cotes (1734-1818) lived from 1794 to 1798, as did the sculptor Edward Hodges Bailey RA (1788-1867) from 1825 to 1828.

George Rowney & Co., established 1783, moved to **No.12** from 51 Rathbone Place in the 1850s. There are two blue plaques nearby: Coventry Patmore (1823-1896), poet and essayist, lived at **No.14** 1863-4 while the actor Charles Laughton (1899-1962) lived at **No.15** from 1928 to 1931, at the time he married Elsa Lanchester and first appeared in British feature films.

Mary Wollstonecraft (p 65) lived briefly at No.26 in 1795 with her newborn baby Fanny Imlay and tried to poison herself. The only house still in domestic use is **No.29**, with the wide black door. It is

2 1740s interior of 29 Percy Street photographed in 1967.

noted for its fine internal decoration of the 1740s (Fig 2).

The uniform effect of the street is broken on this side by 1960s development after No.28, as far as the corner with Tottenham Court Road. This was the scene of one of a series of explosions in gas mains which took place on 17 July 1880 when a stand pipe was tested with a naked flame (the foreman was castigated for carelessness at the subsequent inquest). Five houses were wrecked, two people died and 400 were injured. However, much more damage was caused during WW II, and this stretch was largely derelict until Metropolis House was erected.

That development created a new street (called Windmill Street) which leads us through to (the original) **WINDMILL STREET**, into which we turn left, with Tottenham Court Road behind us. Since Tudor times there had existed a farm track to the windmill there. In 1601, the windmill is recorded as breaking during a 'great tempest'. Building leases were sold on the south side as early as 1723-4, but most houses were not completed until the 1760s.

The street has some interesting associations with charitable organisations. In 1747 the Westminster French Charity school was opened here, still going strong 50 years later, and in 1776 the St Pancras Orphanage and Female Charity School was founded at No.12 before moving to 108 Hampstead Road in 1790. More

famous than either was the **Middlesex Hospital**, founded (as were many of London's most famous hospitals) on the initiative of private citizens during the second quarter of the 18th century.

'Middlesex Infirmary' opened in August 1745, in Nos.8 and 10 Windmill Street (rented from Mr Goodge), to meet the needs of the sick and the lame of Soho and St Giles, four out of five of whose inhabitants were marked with smallpox. The name was changed to Middlesex Hospital in November 1746, and from June 1747 midwifery cases were taken, the inscription outside reading "The Middlesex Hospital For Sick and Lame and Lying-in Women". As the need for space increased land was bought in Marylebone Fields, and patients were transferred to the present hospital, in what is now the borough of Westminster, in 1757.

At No.6 the *Club Autonomie*, an anarchist club, met in the early 1890s and was often raided by police.

Walk across to the **Fitzroy Tavern** at the corner of **CHARLOTTE STREET**. The present building, built in 1897, was designed in exotic turn-of-the-century style by W M Brutton, a prolific pub architect. In the 1920s and 1930s this was an artists' meeting place, especially for the circle around Augustus John, who remarked that a man who hadn't been to the Fitzroy hadn't been to London. A younger crowd (which included Dylan Thomas) emigrated

to The Wheatsheaf in Rathbone Place when there got to be too many 'tourists' and hangers-on. Daniel Farson in his book on Soho recalls The Fitzroy Tavern's exotic days in the 1950s when police raided the place because of its many "perverts" but they lost the subsequent prosecution against the long-standing publican, Charles Allchild. His daughter, Sally Fiber, has recently written a fascinating account of the characters who frequented the pub.

Just down from the opposite corner, at **No.8** Charlotte Street, now *Chez Gérard*, Richard Wilson (1714-1783), the 'father of English landscape painting', lived from 1773 to 1779. Across Charlotte Street at **Nos.15-17** is a grand Victorian building which replaced the Percy Chapel. Since 1923 it has been home to Cottrell's, denture manufacturer, who bought the two large gas lamps outside the main entrance to save them from destruction. Next door, Nos.19-21 is **Bertorelli's**, an example of Fitzrovia's strong Italian links. It was founded in 1913 by two brothers from Italy, one of whom (Giuseppe) died at the grand old age of 101 in 1995. At first it catered for the local working class, but the café became popular with writers during the 1920s and 1930s. The family left in 1984, but the name was retained.

Walking northwards we pass on our right a good row of 18th-century houses, the best being **No.26**, noted by Pevsner. At

No.30, the French restaurant *L'Etoile* was founded in 1906, in a house formerly occupied by Charles Dibdin (1745-1814), dramatist and song writer. This was one of the street's first restaurants, which have proliferated since the 1930s. Another old restaurant, this time a German one, was at Nos.33-43, now the Villa Carlotta, opposite us on the corner of Rathbone Street. This was *Schmidt's*, set up as a sausage shop in 1901 when this area was the German quarter of London. Herr Schmidt started the restaurant after WW I, in which he had served as a British army cook. The family never advertised, but Schmidt's was open every day of the year until it closed in July 1975.

We soon reach busy **GOODGE STREET**. The **Northumberland Arms** to our left dates back to 1766-7, when Francis and William Goodge launched their most ambitious scheme, a new shopping thoroughfare across Crabtree Fields, from Tottenham Court Road towards Middlesex Hospital. By 1770 the street was inhabited by the kind of tradesmen associated with Fitzrovia for the next 200 years: carpenters, oilmen, ironmongers and tobacconists. In 1838 Tallis called it "a broad and open street of great thoroughfare, entirely composed of respectable retail shops". The area declined in status after that; there was a street market on Friday and Saturday nights in Victorian times. By the turn of the century there was a mixed community of Jewish, Irish, English, French and Italian people, increasingly displaced after 1945 by cafés and restaurants. However, a good range of shops remains.

Turn right into Goodge Street and note the stretch of original 18th-century four-storey houses, with a modillioned cornice unifying what was planned as a single design, although the end houses each with a pediment in place of the upper range of windows have since gone.

Walk along the street to the Goodge Street Underground station on Tottenham Court Road, or continue the walk along Route 1B.

Around central Fitzrovia

From Goodge Street Underground station turn right and right again into Goodge Street, then take the second right into the northern part of Charlotte Street, where many of the original houses have been replaced. However, as you cross **SCALA STREET** look right: on its south side there is a run of original 18th-century houses, two with pedimented porticoes to the doors. The street name recalls the Scala Theatre (*see below*), which stood behind the offices of Cable TV company Channel One, **No.60**.

Make a brief detour to the right down **TOTTENHAM STREET** to see **Nos. 30-24**, on the north side, original four-storeyed 18th-century houses. No.30 is unusual because the wooden frames to the windows are virtually flush to the wall, which building regulations forbade at this time (the late 1760s) in more central parts of London. These houses face a modern development on what was once the entrance to the Scala Theatre, the last of a long line of theatrical establishments here, starting with a concert room in 1772 and including the Prince of Wales Theatre 1865-1882, where Ellen Terry often performed. Demolished in 1902, it was

rebuilt in 1904 as the Scala Theatre, designed by Francis T Verity, the theatre's name referring to the striking inside staircase (p 22). The earliest hand-coloured films and the first screening of *Birth of A Nation* could be seen here when it was used as a cinema in 1911-1913. During

---

Street names along route 1B and their origin

Charlotte
George III's queen
Chitty
family of Victorian legal writers
Cleveland
Charles II's mistress was created Duchess of Cleveland, and their descendant Charles Fitzroy, 4th duke of Grafton, developed his estate of Tottenham Court
Colville
John Colvill was Goodge family's carpenter
Howland
Duke of Bedford is also Baron Howland
Rathbone
Thomas Rathbone inherited a house here
Scala
a theatre was reconstructed here in 1904 with dramatic internal stairway
Tottenham
From Tottenham Court
Whitfield
Rev George Whitefield was minister of Methodist chapel in Tottenham Court Road

---

WW II it was home to the US Army Theatre Unit. After that it was famous for its annual production of *Peter Pan*. The Beatles' concert here in 1964 formed the basis for their film *A Hard Day's Night*. The theatre closed in 1969.

Back in **CHARLOTTE STREET**, to our left on the west side at **Nos.77-79** is a building in somewhat nautical style - chrome rails, shades of blue and green, and an aluminium canopy. It houses another Cable TV company, *The Sci-Fi Channel*. This building results from a radical overhaul of a 1960s office block which in 1989 was stripped back to its original concrete frame to carry a new façade. Next door at **No.81** is a plain 18th-century house. The blue plaque tells us this was once home to the architect Sir Robert Smirke (1781-1867), designer of the British Museum, who spent most of his childhood here (1786-1804) with his painter father Robert.

Further north on the east side, No.72 has an old shop front with its original wood casing. Two doors along is the post-modern **Ariel House**, built 1991. It stands on the site of St John the Evangelist, consecrated in July 1846, whose Romanesque style offended the Gothic purists writing in the contemporary periodical *The Ecclesiologist*. The Rev Charles Kingsley, author of *The Water Babies*, preached a subversive sermon here in 1851 blaming the rich for the sufferings

of the poor. Badly damaged by a flying bomb in 1945, it was demolished in the 1960s.

Also demolished was No.76, where Joseph Farington (1747- 1821), a landscape painter (and diarist) who had studied under Richard Wilson, lived 1783-1821. Soon after his death his friend John Constable moved in. Constable had lived almost opposite at No.63, now 85, from 1811 to 1817 (p 26). Constable always spent his summers in Hampstead; however, it was not in Hampstead but here in his painting studio, "light, airy, sweet and warm", that he did most of his paintings, including *Salisbury Cathedral*. He died in the little attic bedroom on 31 March 1837.

Do not pursue Charlotte Street further northwards, where modern flats and offices have replaced the old terraces. One of the vanished houses was No.82; here the opera singer Angelica Catalani (1779-1849) lived in 1810. She is said to have been the highest-paid opera singer in history. Her legendary greed was one cause of the several-month-long 'Old Price' riots at Covent Garden in 1809 over increased seat prices. She was caricatured as 'Mrs Catsqualani' by Rowlandson.

With the Telecom Tower towering

3 Staircase of the Scala Theatre (F T Verity, 1904).

ahead on the left, turn right into **CHITTY STREET**, renamed from North Street in 1885 in honour of the Chitty family (father and two sons), all distinguished Victorian legal writers. All here is now uninspiring 20th-century development.

Turn right into **WHITFIELD STREET** (formerly John Street). It never achieved the social status of neighbouring Charlotte Street, possibly because of the poor quality of the houses. The west side of Tottenham Court Road was long used as an ash tip by Londoners, and this provided a source for the bricks made on site and put together with mud from nearby pools and puddles! This was discovered when the basement of the building housing Pollock's Toy Museum had to be shored up in 1975.

Behind the trees to our left is the back of the Methodist chapel dedicated to the memory of George Whitefield [sic], after whom this street is now named. Turn left into a rather seedy open place, which used to be part of the burial grounds surrounding the chapel. In 1798 a band of body snatchers was intercepted here, the area already being associated with the 'resurrection men'. The grounds became a health hazard and were closed in 1853. After protracted struggles with would-be developers it became a public park in 1895.

Circle round to the right (avoiding Tottenham Court Road) and look at the elaborate mural on the side wall of No.8

Tottenham Street, painted in 1981 by the Arts Workers Co-op for the Fitzrovia community.

Cross Tottenham Street (this portion was known as Chapel Street when it was developed in the late 1760s) towards **The Hope** pub, noting that at No.13 at the opposite corner, Olaudah Equiano, otherwise Gustavus Vasa, former slave and prominent abolitionist, and a founding member of the London Corresponding Society, lived in 1788. At The Hope, a peculiar building with an attractive first-floor corner window, turn left down Whitfield Street again.

A few doors away from the corner of Scala Street to our right is **Pollock's Toy Museum** and shop, selling toy theatres. Founded in 1851 in Hoxton where it remained until bombed in WW II, the museum moved here (via Seven Dials) in 1969. Robert Louis Stevenson wrote "If you love art, folly or the bright eyes of children, speed to Pollock's".

On the opposite corner, at No.39, is the **Café Cyberia**, the first in the world offering dedicated access to the Internet. Founded in September 1994, it now has branches in Paris, Tokyo and New York.

The east side of the street was much damaged in WW II. Here dwelt the Literary and Scientific Institution, founded by followers of Robert Owen, from 1840 to 1858. Its galleried, spacious hall was an important meeting place for radical

political groups and emergent Trades Unions. The Chartists met here on 15 April 1848, when Feargus O'Connor tried unsuccessfully to persuade them not to take their petition in procession to Parliament. In 1851 Mrs Knight advocated bloomers for women here so they might run, jump and dance like men.

Across Goodge Street we arrive on our right at the start of **COLVILLE PLACE**. These pleasant gardens were developed on a former bomb site, which until the 1980s served as a car park. The ground was compulsorily purchased by the GLC in 1985 after much community pressure. A year later the park was created and named Crabtree Fields, the original name of the area.

At the west side of the Place, a paved residential court has small three-storeyed terraced houses. Planned in 1766 by William Franks, it was built by the younger Goodges' carpenter John Colvill, who lived here until 1783. Some still have early-19th-century shop fronts, and all appear very spruce, bedecked with plants and flowers, some with roof gardens, a far cry from 1878 when the penniless George Gissing lodged here at the now destroyed No.22. He later wrote *New Grub Street*, making many references to the then grim area west of Tottenham Court Road.

Emerging in Charlotte Street cross left and turn right into **RATHBONE STREET** by the side of the Villa Carlotta. The **Duke of York** pub at the end marks

the boundary with Westminster. It is little altered externally since it was erected in the 1760s. Alf Klein, landlord from 1938 until his death in 1964, was known as the Mad Major: he liked to cut off his customers' ties and collected some 1500 of them!

Turn right there into **CHARLOTTE PLACE**, another paved court, probably originally with two rows of three-storey houses, erected 1766-67 again under William Franks' direction. Several to our right have been rebuilt and are now four storeys high, with shops on the ground floor.

At the end we reach Goodge Street once more. A brief detour to our left takes us to **Nos.59 & 61**, each bearing an old parish boundary marker. Goodge Street was the scene of a famous attempt to resuscitate the hanged Rev William Dodd (1729-1777), a favourite of society ladies and known as the 'macaroni preacher', who was executed at Tyburn for forging a £4,200 bond in the name of the Earl of Chesterfield. His body was taken to an undertaker's, where the eminent surgeon John Hunter tried unsuccessfully to revive him.

Return and cross Goodge Street and enter **GOODGE PLACE** opposite. Goodge Place is a cobbled street, still paved with granite setts, and largely as

4 The Charlotte Street house once inhabited by John Constable, photographed in 1947.

originally built in the 1760s (except for the curious monstrosity at Nos.17-18). Unusually, Fourth Rate houses (Georgian building standards) have survived here almost unaltered both internally and externally, probably because alteration has been discouraged by multiple occupancy. By the mid-19th century they were very overcrowded and considered slums. Threatened with demolition since the 1950s, the street has in recent years been renovated, one house here being advertised in 1987 for £240,000. Other houses in the street are now Grade II listed.

At the far end on the right hand corner with Tottenham Street is the Fitzrovia Neighbourhood Centre, opened in 1975. Turn left and pass **No.49**, in the basement of which the Communist Working Men's Club met from 1878 to 1902. Marx, Engels and William Morris were frequent visitors. Note another parish boundary marker on the wall here.

CLEVELAND STREET, which we now reach, has a multifunctional boundary running down the middle of the street: between the Southampton and Portland estates, the old parishes of St Pancras and St Marylebone, and now between the boroughs of Camden and Westminster. J T Smith in his *Book For A Rainy Day* recalls how in the mid-1770s a rope walk shaded by 'two magnificent rows of Elms' extended north along what was then Green Lane as far as Farthing Pie House (the

Green Man on the Euston Road). The painter Richard Wilson often walked under these elms.

The street was developed very gradually from south to north, and was originally purely residential. Over the years it has suffered from the expansion of the Middlesex Hospital opposite, which replaced a terrace of houses, which included No.19. Here in July 1889 the police uncovered a homosexual brothel, largely staffed by Post Office telegraph boys. This became a major public scandal because it was frequented by an Equerry to the Prince of Wales, Lord Arthur Somerset. A warrant for his arrest was issued but he fled, probably with the collusion of the Prime Minister, to Paris. Many other high-ranking people were said to be implicated, including the local landowner Lord Euston and Prince Albert Victor (Eddy), eldest son of the Prince of Wales, who was conveniently in India when the scandal broke. Eddy already had a connection with Cleveland Street. A few years earlier he had formed a liaison with Annie Elizabeth Cook, who worked in a tobacconist's shop at No.20 to our left. She gave birth to his illegitimate daughter in 1885 and he apparently married her in secret soon after. Annie was sent to a mental institution in 1888; her friend Mary Kelly escaped with the baby to the East End but she was later murdered there by Jack The Ripper.

If we look left, Nos.16, 18 and 20 are good examples of early-19th-century shops, with bowed windows and patterned fanlights to the entrances. **No.16** is especially interesting, as it retains a (much decayed) wooden overhang. The café on the corner where we are standing (**No.22**) was Charles Dickens' first London home (as a child) and he returned to live here for two years from 1829.

If we now turn right and walk northwards, beyond the university's Courtauld Institute of Biochemistry (1927) on the corner of Foley Street, to our right is the **King & Queen** pub in an ornate Victorian Gothic style. In the 19th century the pub was an official house of call for the Alliance of Cabinet Makers, and used as a Trade Union library.

Opposite, behind the brick walls to our right, the boxy four-storey brick building, now the Middlesex Hospital Outpatients' Department, was formerly a workhouse built in 1775- 78 for the parish of St Paul's, Covent Garden on land given by the Duke of Bedford, the site of an old burial ground. In 1829 it was enlarged as the Strand Union Workhouse and from 1874 became the Central London Sick Asylum Infirmary. Since 1927 it has been the Middlesex Hospital Annexe.

At the corner with Howland Street is the Windeyer Building of the Middlesex Hospital Medical School (1957-62). This covers the site of St Mary's Lutheran

Church, destroyed in WW II, and the house in which the Pre-Raphaelite Brotherhood was founded in 1848. Dante Gabriel Rossetti (1828-1882) and Holman Hunt (1824-1910) rented a studio here in autumn 1848. Hunt introduced Rossetti to John Millais (1829-1896), with whom he had studied at the Royal Academy, and together they started the Brotherhood. Hunt fell behind with the rent and Rossetti then moved to 27 Newman Street, directly to the south.

At this point you can either turn right into Howland Street to regain Tottenham Court Road with its Underground and (northbound) bus stops, or continue with the walk in section 1C. **HOWLAND STREET** was built on Culver Meadow, land owned by the Bedford Estate. Wriothesley Russell, son of William Lord Russell, married Elizabeth, daughter of John Howland of Streatham, in 1695, when (curiously) not he but his grandfather, the 5th earl and 1st duke of Bedford, received the title **Baron Howland of Streatham** added to the others - Marquess of Tavistock and Duke of Bedford (instead of earl) - bestowed on him by William and Mary the previous year. Perhaps the barony came to his grandfather because Wriothesley was only 15 when he married. All the titles duly descended to him on his grandfather's death in 1700. This field of 12 acres was developed 1776-91 by William Gowing.

Very little of the original development remains after extensive war damage, so that Howland Street today contains only modern office blocks.

Northern Fitzrovia (from Howland Street to Warren Street Tube station)

Walk west from Tottenham Court Road along Howland Street to the corner of Cleveland Street, and turn right (north) along the latter. As far as Maple Street the block on the east side is taken up by the buildings at the foot of the Telecom Tower, which was completed in 1966 (then the 'Post Office Tower'), to support aerials for radio, television and telephone transmission. The tower is 620 feet high and was the tallest building in London until the National Westminster Tower was finished in 1981. When first built it was widely admired for its pure, 'innocent' engineering. The observation gallery has been closed since the early 1970s after an IRA bomb explosion there.

MAPLE STREET (named after the furniture store family) was laid out for building (as London Street) in 1777-8. The north side was in the Southampton estate. From here to the Euston Road stretched the Home Field, the last area of Fitzrovia to be built up, at the end of the 18th century. The Home Field was part of Tottenhall manor, held in Charles II's time by the Earl of Arlington.

His daughter Isabella was married, aged 5, to the King's natural son, Henry **Fitzroy**, first Duke of **Grafton**, and the manor was later settled on their great-grandson Charles Fitzroy, created Lord

Street names along route 1C and their origin

Conway
Isabella Lady Conway was a great-granddaughter of 2nd duke of Grafton

Euston
Estate in Suffolk brought to duke of Grafton by marriage to daughter of Lord Arlington

Fitzroy
Henry Fitzroy, second son of Charles II and Duchess of Cleveland, was created Duke of Grafton.
The fourth duke, Charles Fitzroy, developed what is now known as Fitzrovia

Grafton
see Fitzroy, above

Hertford
Lady Conway was also Marchioness of Hertford

Maple
Founder of the furnishing firm

Warren
Anne Warren married Charles Fitzroy, 4th Duke of Grafton and 1st Baron Southampton

Whitfield
Rev George Whitefield was minister of Methodist chapel in Tottenham Court Road

Southampton in 1780. He married Anne, daughter of Admiral Sir Peter **Warren**. At this western end of Maple Street, much of which suffered badly in WW II, a few of the original terraced houses on the north side remain, somewhat down at heel. In the stretch to our right the original railings are extant and **Nos.46** and **48** have brackets supporting wooden hoods.

Some way down Maple Street, there is a pub at the corner of Fitzroy Street by the traffic lights. This was formerly the *Yorkshire Grey*, but now bears the strange name the **Prince Monolulu**. Prince Ras Monolulu (1881-1965) lived in Cleveland Street. Born in Ethiopia, said to be the son of a chieftain (Fig 5), and sometimes known as Peter McKay, he was a tipster at the races and at Petticoat Lane, often loudly dressed in colourful garb with a feather head-dress. Maple Street was also the site of the Fitzroy Chapel opened in December 1778, a rather plain chapel of ease renamed the Church of St Saviour in 1863 and destroyed in 1945.

Returning to Cleveland Street and continuing northwards, we pass **Nos.66-82** (best seen as original 18th-century from the opposite, Marylebone, side of the street) and, later, a three-storey late-18th-century terrace (Nos.100-126) with mansard roofs and some original wood features. **No.106** is particularly impressive, with its elaborate bowed shop front of very delicate carving.

Opposite us on the Westminster side of the street there is a plaque at **No.141** to Samuel Morse, American painter and inventor of the Morse Code, who lived in this house in 1812-15.

5 'Prince Monolulu' with his Ethiopian grandfather, 1965.

Just before Cleveland Street ends in the traffic roar of Euston Road, turn right into **WARREN STREET**. This was built, mainly in 1790-92, as a residential street of three-storey houses in stock brick. Once popular with artists and literary men, it went downhill in the 19th century, and for unknown reasons became from the 1930s a centre for second-hand car sales. It has recently been largely rehabilitated.

At **No.43** (now part of an office block, Nos.40-50) lived from 1817 until his death the eccentric Dr Kitchiner (1775-1827), famous at the time for his theories on household management and dining (eg oysters for health). **No.50**, also rebuilt, was the home for over half a century of Charles Turner (1774-1857), the mezzotint engraver, but he lived previously at **No.56**, which bears a plaque. On the other side of the street, at the southwest corner with Conway Street, note what used to be the shop of J Evans, dairy farmer, the name emblazoned in Victorian gold lettering surrounded by superb lustrous blue tiling.

Turn south down **CONWAY STREET** (Hampstead Street until 1884, then Southampton Street until 1938), an attractive residential street of late-18th-century four-storey houses. **Nos.14-20** on the east side date from 1793, stuccoed at ground floor level, their long first-floor balconies having interlaced gothic ironwork. The similar houses on the west side date from 1798 onwards. The street opens up into the architectural highlight of the walk, **FITZROY SQUARE**. Many tempting benches surround this splendid square, most of it pedestrianised.

The square was begun in the 1790s, but remained a long time unfinished; the north and west sides were not begun until the late 1820s and the early 1830s respectively. We shall walk down the west side, which affords the best view of the stone-faced east

6A Robert Adam design for the east side of Fitzroy Square, instantly recognisable in the modern Square.

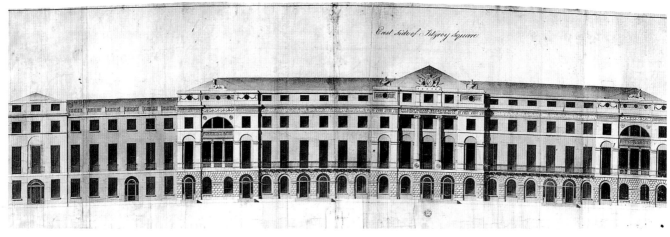

and south sides which were designed by Robert Adam (1728-1792); the stuccoed houses on the north and west sides, while pleasing, are not in the same league. It is worth remembering that when this square was erected the surrounding district was already built up; the traditional method of making the bricks on site gave rise to considerable complaints from respectable residents nearby. Like much of Fitzrovia it declined in status during the 19th century and was really quite seedy by 1900, with several commercial hotels offering cheap rooms. Since World War II it has been smartened up, but taken over by offices.

6B Adam's south side of Fitzroy Square.

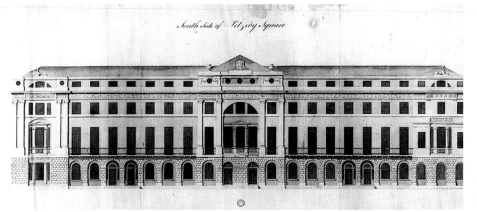

Across the square from where we stand, the **east side** was begun in 1792-93. Adam had designed (Fig 6A) an imposing range of 11 buildings, four storeys high plus a basement, each with a 24-foot frontage. The main structural feature is a Portland stone façade with three projecting sections. The rusticated ground floor contains a series of arches within which the doors and windows are set. At **No.2** William Dyce (1806-1864), the Pre-Raphaelite painter, lived from 1853 to 1869. There are blue plaques at **No.7** for Charles Eastlake (1793-1865), artist and first director of the National Gallery, who lived there from

1844 to 1855 and at **No.10**, where A W Hofmann (1818-1892), the German professor who spent 20 years in London founding a school of industrial chemistry in England, lived from 1854 to 1865. The Georgian Group is now based at No.6.

The **north side** was started in 1827-28 and contained nine houses. There is a modern central insertion: **No.14** housing St Luke's Hospital for Clergy (which moved here in 1907) and No.13, both recently refaced in grey stone. Nos.15 and 16 show remnants of the original central feature with shallow flat Ionic pilasters embracing the second and third storeys, surmounted by a palmetted frieze. **No.14** was home from 1871 to 1900 to Robert William Edis (1838-1927), an architect known as 'The Colonel', who designed several railway stations such as at Liverpool Street.

Continue along the **west side**, for which building leases for 13 houses were granted from 1832 to 1835. The whole range is faced in stucco, the design reflecting the east side in its projecting features. Most notable is the house in the centre, with its four tall Ionic attached columns carrying the entablature. Robert Gascoigne Cecil (1830-1903), later 3rd Marquis of Salisbury and Prime Minister, lived for a short while at **No.21**, where in 1909 John Maynard Keynes and Duncan Grant shared rooms. The bronze plaque on **No.29** records that George Bernard Shaw

(1856-1950) lived here 1887-98 and 'from the coffers of his genius he enriched the world'. This was when he was still a struggling young playwright and critic, supported by his mother. The blue plaque below tells us that Virginia Stephen (later Woolf) (1882-1941) also lived here, in 1907-11, when she hosted regular readings.

The **south side** of eight houses, started in 1794, is a very satisfying composition (p 31). Its treatment is like the east, and the central feature containing a large thermal window is based on that side's end projections, but the wings and central block are narrower because of the shorter length. Nos.36 and 38, including the centre, were completely destroyed in WW II but have been successfully re-created. This side has important artistic links. In 1913 Roger Fry established the **Omega Workshops**, to introduce Post-Impressionist ideas into England, at **No.33**, now part of the London Foot Hospital which occupies both ends. At **No.37** Ford Madox Brown (1821-1893), a painter with a strong influence on the Pre-Raphaelites, lived from 1867 to 1882, regularly entertaining Rossetti, Burne-Jones, Holman Hunt and William Morris there. At **No.40** William Frend de Morgan (1839-1917) artist, inventor and novelist, best known for his ceramic tiles, began his experiments, but having set fire to the roof of his house he decided to move to

Chelsea. Here the London Skin Hospital was housed from 1891 to 1948.

At the eastern end of the south side, just round the corner in Fitzroy Street on the wall to your right, is a bronze statue of Francisco de Miranda (1750-1816), pioneer of Latin American independence. He led a rebellion in Venezuela against Spain, where he was to die a prisoner. Before this he had lived 1802-10 at No.58 Grafton Way (plaques to Miranda and his fellow fighter Andres Bello), which leads out of Fitzroy Square.

Before pursuing Grafton Way, glance down **FITZROY STREET**, which runs for only two blocks before becoming Charlotte Street but which has over the years housed a host of well-known artists (W P Frith, S F Gore, Walter Sickert, Sir William Coldstream, Augustus John) as well as other famous people (Octavia Hill, Vanessa Bell, Duncan Grant, the explorer Matthew Flinders and Dylan Thomas). Sickert formed the **Fitzroy Street Group** of artists in 1907. They held shows at No.19 and here Sickert, his friend Harold Gilman and others formed the Camden Town Group in Spring 1911; these linked with the Vorticists in 1913 to become The London Group. Sickert himself moved to various addresses in Camden Town, West Hampstead and Holborn but returned in 1915 to No.8 (where Whistler formerly had had a studio) and then No.15. These terraces survived World War II but not the

developers: they have been replaced by tall office blocks.

The south side of **GRAFTON WAY** is taken up with the Indian YMCA building, designed in 1952 by Ralph Tubbs. It covers the site of the home in 1793-97 of Gainsborough's nephew and only pupil, Gainsborough Dupont, who died here aged just 30. On the north side the **Grafton Arms** is an attractive pub which dates back to the start of the street, and beyond this is a good row of 18th-century houses, including No.58.

As we turn left into **WHITFIELD STREET** note on the right No.108, **Marie Stopes House**. Marie Stopes moved her 'Mothers' Clinic for Constructive Birth Control' here from Holloway in 1925 four years after it was founded. The clinic here still offers family planning, health screening and specialist gynaecological services.

The northernmost section of Whitfield Street was originally called Hertford Street (and the name lingers in HERTFORD PLACE, a sort of mews lying west of Whitfield Street between Grafton and Maple Streets). Most of the formerly celebrated early-19th-century shop fronts on the west side of Whitfield Street have either collapsed or been demolished, except for **Nos. 131, 135 & 137**. At No.137 Khan's, one of the first Indian restaurants in London, opened in 1945. The terrace has been reconstructed.

No. 145 bears a plaque commemorating the first settlement of the Nepali community in 1965.

On the east side is a public open space. This was once the site of Fitzroy Market, a typical example of the shopping centres planned in connection with new residential schemes in the Georgian period. It had open stalls surrounded by small shops, which degenerated into very poor housing during the 19th century. It was later replaced by public swimming baths with wash-house, built in an outlandish Moorish style. The baths opened in May 1878 and survived until WW II. The site then became a car park until a fund-raising campaign enabled it to become the **Warren Playground**, opened in 1979 by Frank Dobson, the local MP.

Turn right into Warren Street again. Across the road is No.65, which became briefly notorious in 1886 during the Crawford divorce case. Mrs Crawford, the wife of a Home Office official, confessed to an affair with Sir Charles Dilke MP, a leading Liberal politician, and said in court that they met here in the house of his former servant. Dilke declined to give evidence and the press had a field day - he was forced to resign as an MP.

On our right just past the **Prince of Wales' Feathers** public house, which was licensed as a theatre in the mid-19th century, is the last remaining car salesroom (founded 1936) in the street. From here to the corner with Tottenham Court Road was an early cinema, The Grafton as it was known from 1911, which opened in November 1910. It closed in 1929, becoming successively a theatre (until 1940) and then a BBC studio for some 20 years.

Cross the road from here to reach Warren Street Underground station and the end of our walk.

Down Tottenham Court Road

Our walk will begin at the northern extremity, Warren Street station, but the history of the road begins at the southern end, where the Roman road from the City of London to the west crossed one running northwards from Westminster. Prior to the 18th century there were just a few inns and farm buildings along Tottenham Court Road from this crossroads northwards as far as present-day Windmill Street, which was then a track to the windmill which was to give the street its name. When George Whitefield's Methodist chapel (p 36) was built midway along this street in 1756 it was on the edge of London, being bordered to the north by fields frequented by highwaymen and other robbers.

From 1760 building proceeded apace, first on the west side of the Road and then on the east. By 1800 buildings reached to the New Road and beyond, along Hampstead Road. The terraces at the northern end were mostly residential, but in the years after 1800 many craftsmen and cabinet makers began to set up workshops there. By the late 19th century it had become London's leading shopping street for furniture, bedding and soft furnishings. It was also one of the first London streets to be provided with electric light, in 1892. Heal's, Maple's, Shoolbred's and Catesby's were just some of the larger stores in 1900. Before WW I it also became lined with picture houses, with no fewer than six by 1913; all of these early cinemas have gone, but there is one modern multi-screen cinema, opposite Bayley Street.

Difficult as it is to visualise as you come out of Warren Street station, it is a fact that just to the north of here the manor of Tottenham Court (originally Totehele Manor) was a favourite rural resort of Londoners from the early 1600s until 200 years later, by which time its surrounding fields had been built over.

Walk south down the west side of **TOTTENHAM COURT ROAD**, noticing the distinctive lamp standards, now painted white, all the way down the middle of the road. These were part of the first electric street lighting in London. Pass the **Grafton Hotel** (No.130), where Lady Ottoline Morrell is said to have spent two nights with Bertrand Russell during their brief affair. Outside No.128 once stood a life-sized dummy Highlander, an old sign of tobacconists, which students in the 19th century regularly used to 'borrow'. Opposite, on the east side, Seifert's overpowering, marble-faced development now houses the Housing Corporation and **Maple's furniture store**. Initially Maple and Cook from 1841, the partnership was dissolved in 1851. It received a grand 'New Delhi' style front by Sir Herbert Baker in 1905, when it was claimed to be the largest furniture establishment in the world. On our side we pass Fitzroy Court (between Nos.126 and 127) with an arcade of lamp holders. When first built, this passageway gave on to the Fitzroy Market in Whitfield Street (p 33), now the Warren Playground.

At the crossing with Grafton Way, Nos.117 and 118 are rare survivors in the street of late-18th-century buildings, now stuccoed. The whole block opposite (Nos.151-162, as far as University Street) was the site of Shoolbred's, founded as a draper's in 1820 and by the 1850s one of the first department stores ever. Pulled down in 1935, the corner with Grafton Way (where the hoardings are) was redeveloped as the Paramount, later Odeon, cinema. This closed in 1960 and was demolished; the site remained empty until 1997 (p 41). The Tallis pictorial map of 1838-40 (Fig 7) shows the previous shops on this site.

Cross Maple Street. Opposite, from Mortimer Market down towards Torrington Place, the newly built houses at the turn of 19th century (all gone) were known as The Terrace. At No.4 once lived the architect George Dance the younger (1740-1828) (see also p 44).

As we cross Howland Street there is a

good view (right) of the Telecom Tower. Further down on the east side, note **Ye Olde Surgeon**, a recent name for The New Inn. In the late 18th century the New Inn was renowned for the dog-fighting pits at the back, which were closed after a prosecution in 1830. From a space nearby, the balloonist Francesco Zambeccari (1756-1806) made an ascent in March 1785, lost control and was blown all the way to Horsham in 60 minutes.

Past the attractive glass-fronted No.85 and set back from the road on our right is a circular concrete building with a "Security Archives" sign. This was the entrance to one of the deep shelters built during WW II and allocated to the American Army (p 67). After the war it was a military transit camp until 1956 and in 1974 was leased to the British Library for the storage of books.

Next, set back behind a few trees, is

Whitefield Memorial Church. The evangelical preacher George Whitefield (1714-1770) was in his day as famous as Wesley, and his ability to attract large crowds alienated him from the Church of England authorities. With the help of supporters like the Countess of Huntingdon he acquired the lease of this site from the Goodge family and built a chapel which opened in November 1756. Whitefield preached here to such large congregations that the building had to be enlarged in 1759. The chapel itself was square in plan with a pyramidal roof topped by a cupola, and could hold up to 4000 people, making it then the largest Nonconformist church in the world. It was derisively known as Whitefield's soul trap, but attracted several leading figures in society, including Lord Chesterfield and Horace Walpole. Whitefield died in America in 1770. John Wesley (with whom he had had doctrinal differences) preached his funeral service in the chapel (p 36), which was decked in mourning for 6 weeks. The Rev Augustus Toplady (d.1778), author of the hymn *Rock of*

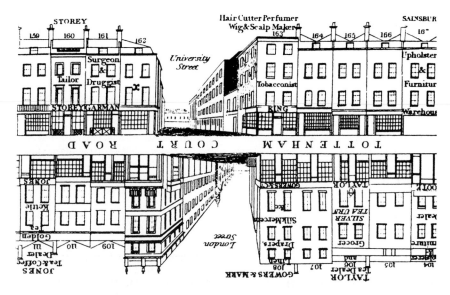

7 Part of Tallis's pictorial map (1838) of Tottenham Court Road, showing the University Street corner which was later the site of Shoolbred's and then the Odeon cinema, demolished in 1960. The site is at last (1997) being redeveloped as part of University College Hospital.

36   8 *The first Whitefield Memorial chapel (T Clark, 1826).*

Ages, was buried in the chapel.

Two subsequent buildings on the site were destroyed by fire or bombing, and the present building dates from 1957. It is the inter-denominational "American Church in London, catering to long- and short-term expatriates"; it also shelters the London Chinese Lutheran Church.

Opposite, at Nos.191-199, is **Heal's store**. John Harris Heal, the founder of the firm, moved to 203 Tottenham Court Road from Rathbone Place in 1818, and his widow carried on the business after he died. Their son John Harris Heal moved to Miller's stables at No.196, backing on Cantelowes Close, still farmland then, and he lived in the 18th-century farmhouse behind. The firm continued to expand, and adjoining properties were bought up.

In 1907 Ambrose Heal became chairman and in 1916 the architects Smith and Brewer built the present premises, demolishing the farmhouse behind. The façade expressed Heal's preoccupation with functional craftsmanship. Stone casings to the steel frame are divided by blue spandrels showing tools of the trade. The curved display windows on the ground floor were ingenious. The shop was extended in 1937 (note the gilded *fasces* on the top floor, betraying the date of the architecture) and again in 1961-62, when a pub on the corner of Torrington Place called *Apollo and the Muses*, a creation of 1898, was demolished.

Heal's always prided themselves on fostering the best in design of furnishings and fabrics, especially when British craftsmen were involved. Its large craft workshops kept the Arts and Crafts movement alive. Early in the 20th century Heal's Mansard Gallery was used for exhibitions of *avant garde* art, for instance Roger Fry, Duncan Grant and Mark Gertler in 1913.

South of the Goodge Street Underground station, look up and admire the exuberant Edwardian building on the corner with Goodge Street. The sculpted C recalls that this was Catesby's, once known as Linoland, Catesby's being advertised as "the home of cork lino". It stands opposite what was once a famous store on the corner of Chenies Street: Hewetson's, one of the oldest furniture firms in the road. Founded in Oxford Street in 1800, the cost of relocating here after a fire forced it to close in 1905.

Crossing Goodge Street and passing the police station, note the block on the corner with Store Street at **Nos.220-225**; it has good rubbed-brick panels of faces between gigantic composite pilasters. A more impressive architectural creation on our side, at the corner with Windmill Street (No.46) is **The Rising Sun**, with sun's rays in its ogee-shaped gables. A pub of this name has been here since at least 1830. The present building dates from 1897 and was designed by Treadwell and

Martin in what Pevsner described as "fanciful Art Nouveau Gothic".

Passing ugly Metropolis House, we get a chance to look right along tree-lined Percy Street (p 19). At the corner, No.38 (and No.20 Percy Street) is an original 1760s building. On the corner of Bayley Street (p 70) almost opposite is the **Bedford Corner Hotel** above the **Jack Horner** pub (No.236). The hotel is Victorian Italianate with arched windows and rich impost mouldings, and elaborate ironwork to the upper windows.

We now walk past the 1970s EMI development, which begins with a triple-screen cinema, the Classic, with an unobtrusive entrance. This is on the site of the Majestic Picturedrome (p 38), one of the first, and then quite the grandest, of the cinemas with which Tottenham Court Road was once replete - there have been cinemas in this street at Nos. 24, 28, 30, 36, 134a, 163, 194, 268 and 269.

Virtually every shop now on both sides of the street sells electronic equipment. Other than window shopping, there is little to detain us until we cross Hanway Street by the Blue Posts pub (p 17). The building immediately opposite, with Boots on the ground floor, was originally The Horseshoe Hotel, designed in French chateau style for the publican Charles Best in 1875. It was for that time an ambitious development combining a pub, restaurant, grill, café and hotel.

Next to it is the Dominion Theatre which opened in 1929 but became a cinema in 1932, replacing an earlier cinema nearby, The Court Playhouse. The latter opened in 1911, but acquired a notorious reputation for sex films before its closure in 1928. Over the years, the Dominion has steered an erratic course between live theatre, huge cinema, wide-screen cinema complex and again live theatre and lavish musicals, which it was staging at the time of writing.

The Dominion Theatre lies on the entrance to the famous Meux's Horseshoe brewery (p 88) which for over 100 years dominated the entrance to Tottenham Court Road. The earliest brewery here had been run by John Hassell. Henry Meux bought the brewery in 1809, and rebuilt it. Meux's moved to Wandsworth in 1905 and the brewery was demolished in 1922.

We have now arrived at Tottenham Court Road Underground station. From here walks 2C1 and 2C2 can take you into the very different area to the east, Bloomsbury.

9 *The Majestic cinema, 36 Tottenham Court Road, opened in 1912. It survived (as La Continentale from 1948) until 1976. The dome was lined with twelve angelic figures.*

Section 2
Bloomsbury

Bloomsbury's early history, from medieval manor to Georgian suburb around 1830, is outlined on pp 8-12. The photograph opposite the title page of this book shows an aerial view of much of Bloomsbury in 1963.

Despite the aristocratic origins of the Bedford estate, its residents in the 19th century were solidly middle-class, and highly respectable. The dukes of Bedford maintained six bar gates, with uniformed gatekeepers, at entrances to the estate to protect residents from undesirable traffic, whether vehicular or pedestrian; anyone unable to show the requisite silver ticket was debarred. Legislation eventually forced removal of the bars, Gower Street becoming a public thoroughfare for the first time in 1893.

By the end of the 19th century Bloomsbury, though far from being the height of fashion, was acknowledged to be an exceedingly pleasant place to live or simply to walk about in, as celebrated in the following 'Spring Song' by John Davidson in the *Pall Mall Magazine* in 1906.

Laburnum and Lilac

What? Russell Square!
There's lilac there!
And Torrington
And Woburn Square
Intrepid don
The season's wear.
In Gordon Square and Euston Square -
There's lilac, there's laburnum there!
In green and gold and lavender
Queen Square and Bedford Square,
All Bloomsbury and all Soho
With every sunbeam gayer grow,
Greener grow and gayer.

Numerous writers, artists and assorted intellectuals were attracted to live, work and make their names in the area, including, of course, the members of the early 20th-century 'group' with which the name Bloomsbury has become indissolubly associated (p 13). The district has long been a centre of learning, home to the British Museum from its creation in the 1750s, to University College since the 1820s, and later to the University of London and several of its Schools and Institutes. Museum and university today dominate much of the Bedford estate, along with the numerous hotels which cluster around the Museum, one of London's busiest tourist honeypots.

Modernisation of the area in the 20th century was slow, most of the grand houses being preserved, though increasingly taken over for office use. In the 1930s the University's controversial Senate House development cut a swathe through the heart of Georgian Bloomsbury. There was considerable bomb damage during WW II, after which the university and other interests made further encroachments into the residential squares.

Plans in the 1980s for an extension to the British Library, involving the clearance of the whole area north of St George's Bloomsbury, met with strong opposition. Planning blight occurred until an alternative site for the library was eventually secured on Euston Road.

Thereafter the story is of conservation and restoration.

Bloomsbury has no official boundaries, but it is generally accepted that its north, west and south sides are formed by Euston Road, Tottenham Court Road and New Oxford Street respectively. The eastern border is more fluid: in the minds of many, Bloomsbury extends as far east as Gray's Inn Road. For the purposes of this book, the eastern boundary is drawn along the Woburn Place-Southampton Row axis, corresponding roughly to the boundary of the Bedford estate. The streets and squares of 'Bloomsbury' east of that line will be the subject of a future companion volume.

Route 2A.1
Between Tottenham Court Road and Gower Street north of Torrington Place

This walk takes the reader from a point opposite Warren Street Tube station at the north end of Tottenham Court Road down the strip of land between it and Gower Street as far as Torrington Place, formerly Francis Street. This latter east-west road formerly marked the boundary between the parishes of St Pancras to the north and St Giles to the south.

The area was arable land until 1800. Gower Street marked, roughly, the western boundary of the Duke of Bedford's land, although he owned a few meadows amongst the several small estates to the west. Of these estates, those of Charles Fitzroy, Baron Southampton (the larger part of which was to the north of what is now the Euston Road) and of Hans Winthrop Mortimer were the most important. Development on these estates was somewhat piecemeal, in contrast to the stately gridiron pattern further east. The parcel of land dealt with in this walk might even be considered a part of Fitzrovia, since much of it belonged to the same manor (Tottenhall) as the northern part of Section 1; however, the great divide of Tottenham Court Road separates it

sufficiently both in distance and character from the western part that we consider it separately. All but a few pockets of the original development have fallen victim to the appetites of commerce or to the expansion of University College and Hospital, so that very little here predates the 20th century.

Enter **BEAUMONT PLACE** (the grandiose name is derived simply from a builder to whom the land was first leased) from Tottenham Court Road. There is little to see here except the back of Maple's department store and the recently modernised office development of Hobson House along Euston Road, then (after the road makes a right turn) the present main building of University College Hospital (UCH), named Cecil Flemming House, after the chairman of the committee which oversaw its construction. The architects were Adams, Holden & Pierson and the building (opened in June 1970) cost £2.6 million, provided by the DHSS. The tall building nearest Gower Street is the Accident and Emergency department, the first such department in England to have its own 'trauma beds' in which the victims of accidental or other violence are treated by specialists for the first 48 hours. The main entrance is in **GRAFTON WAY** (one of the few roads which continues across the main road from Fitzrovia and retains its name), into which we now turn.

On the other corner with Gower Street

Street names along route 2A.1 and their origin

Beaumont
Joseph Beaumont leased the site in 1791

Capper
Local dairy farming family

Chenies
Chenies, Bucks was brought into the Russell family by the marriage of Anne Sapcote to John Russell, 1st Earl of Bedford

Francis
Christian name of 9th Duke of Bedford

Grafton
Duke of Grafton owned Tottenham manor

Hills
Hills' car numberplate factory was here

Huntley
Second wife of 6th Duke of Bedford was granddaughter of Marquess of Huntly

Mortimer
H W Mortimer MP owned small estate here

Thornhaugh
Another of Anne Sapcote's estates

Torrington
Lord Torrington's daughter was first wife of 6th Duke of Bedford

we see Alfred Waterhouse's striking University College Hospital building (constructed 1896-1905). The first hospital on this site, the North London

Hospital, was built 1833-1836 on land owned by the university; it changed its name to University College Hospital in 1837. The shape of Waterhouse's replacement is at first sight very strange, being in the form of a Greek cross with a central block and four radiating arms. Pevsner, no friend of Waterhouse, observed severely that "the plan breaks the harmony of the street as much as the jagged architecture". The plan was in fact the idea of a doctor, to maximise the amount of light in the wards while improving drainage and sanitation by putting bathrooms at the ends of the arms. After the new UCH was opened in the 1970s the building remained empty for some years; it is currently being refurbished as research laboratories and modern teaching facilities.

Turn back along Grafton Way, and notice the large car park at the corner with Tottenham Court Road, known as the 'Odeon site' (see also p 34) because a 1930s cinema formerly stood there. The empty space is not the result of bombing but of planning blight: although the hospital bought the site in 1960 its development into a further hospital unit had to wait till 1997 to get started. East of the site stands the Rosenheim building, named after Sir Max Rosenheim, professor of medicine in the early 1930s; this contains the private patients' wing, opened by the Duke of Kent in 1936.

Running south from Grafton Way is **HUNTLEY STREET**, named Upper Thornhaugh Street until 1828. This brings us to **UNIVERSITY STREET**, originally Carmarthen Street because it was intended to lead to Carmarthen Square, the projected development on the land which University College London (UCL) eventually occupied (p 43). On the south side stands UCL's **Rayne Institute for Medical Research**, built with funds provided by the Foundation established by the property tycoon Sir Max Rayne, and opened in 1977 by the Queen Mother. The eastern end of the street runs between Waterhouse's UCH and the north side of UCL/UCH Medical School, 1903-7, with colossal Ionic columns. For legal reasons, the Medical School had to be detached from the university in 1907, but was reunited with it in 1980; now it is administratively combined with the medical schools of the Royal Free and Middlesex Hospitals.

One of the pubs in this street, previously the Duke of Wellington, is now named after Jeremy Bentham (1748-1832), who is often credited with the foundation of UCL, though at the age of 78 his role was probably more a philosophical than an active one.

Further down Huntley Street, on the left, stands the Rockefeller nurses' home, built with funds from the Rockefeller Foundation. A grateful **R** has been carved in a pediment on the building's façade, but

the building is a somewhat inconsequential jumble of mostly classical motifs; it is exactly contemporaneous with the singularly dreary maternity hospital opposite, also paid for by the Rockefeller Foundation. Both were opened by the Prince of Wales at the end of May 1926, 3 years after his father had laid the foundation stone for the nurses' home.

Turn right and right again, and you enter **MORTIMER MARKET**. H W Mortimer, MP for Shaftesbury 1774-90, was a property speculator who in 1800 developed his small estate here as a mixture of shops and housing. Praised by Pevsner as a 'humble but remarkable composition', it was one of the few areas in Bloomsbury to contain any purple (working class) on Booth's 1934 poverty map. As it was much damaged during World War II, the university and hospital soon swallowed it up. Where Mortimer's modest shops and street market once stood is now the Mortimer Market Centre (1994), a clinical facility incorporating the UCH Dental Hospital which closed in 1992.

CAPPER STREET, originally Pancras Street, was renamed in 1886 after the dairy-farming Capper family, owners of the meadow called Bromfield until bought out by Mortimer in 1768. They farmed a much wider area as tenants of the Duke of Bedford, from whom they are believed to have rented a farmhouse to the north of Great Russell Street. In 1813 the street was home to a temporary theatre in which one of the actors was Junius Brutus Booth; he later fathered two actor sons, including the John Wilkes Booth who assassinated President Lincoln in 1865.

On the south side, the **Royal Ear Hospital** (opened in 1927 and now known as the Huntley Centre) is worth a glance for its cheery art deco frontage, a world removed from the sulks of the maternity hospital nearby. The rest of the south side is occupied by **Shropshire House**, a block of offices which also houses UCH's department of medical physics and clinical engineering.

Back in Huntley Street, we are pleasantly surprised by a row of early 19th-century houses on the east side, a rare survival of the original development in this area. George Gissing is said to have lived for a time at **No.70**. The houses have been converted into flats for hospital staff. Go through the archway into **CHENIES MEWS** (Chenies, Bucks came into the Russell family early in the 16th century and continues to be cherished as their burial place even though the principal seat has long been the far grander Woburn Abbey) and note the original cobblestone paving. Here in this grimy alleyway some hospital research departments (eg Obstetrics) as well as university works and estates offices have their abode. There is evidence here of former industrial activity: the passageway through which you have just come, **HILLS PLACE**, is named after Hills' car numberplate factory which looms on your right, terminating in a mahogany doorway, somewhat the worse for wear, still labelled *Carpenters*: this formerly led to a firm of cabinet-makers supplying the furniture trade in Tottenham Court Road. An unnumbered, unobtrusive black doorway opposite was formerly the headquarters of the Magic Circle.

Turning right into Torrington Place one passes Huntley Street again, on each corner of which stand turn-of-the-century flats known as Gordon Buildings. For the most part plain and unadorned, they carry high up on the façades unexpected Pont Street Dutch pediments and, at one point, carved winged griffins.

Continuing along **TORRINGTON PLACE** (until 1938 at this western end *Francis* Street), we make our way back to Tottenham Court Road, noting the solid mass of **Mullard House** on our right, yet another outpost of the ubiquitous university and housing the Bartlett School of Architecture, Building, Environmental Design and Planning, as well as further administrative departments of UCL.

In an area where old and new seem inextricably mixed, it is not surprising to learn that as late as the 1960s Torrington Place, together with Huntley Street and Capper Street, formed a turning point for trolley buses.

Across Tottenham Court Road and slightly to the left is Goodge Street Underground station.

Route 2A.2
Northern Gower Street to Upper Woburn Place

This walk lies entirely in the old borough of St Pancras, which was bounded on the south by Torrington Place and its eastward extension. It includes University College London (UCL) and some beautiful houses by the pioneering master-builder Thomas Cubitt (1788-1855) in Gordon and Tavistock Squares.

Starting from Euston Square Underground station we enter the northern end of **GOWER STREET** whose numbering starts from the other end, at Bedford Square. The street named after the wife of the 4th Duke of Bedford marks, roughly, the western boundary of the Bedford estate in Bloomsbury.

For the moment we confine our attention to the eastern (left) side of the street, where there is not much to detain us until we cross Gower Place and encounter University College London (UCL). The land here was bought by a builder in 1824 from the H W Mortimer estate (p 41) with the intention of creating a residential Carmarthen Square, but within a year three benefactors bought him out in order to construct UCL there. Here, unlike at Oxford or Cambridge, neither teachers nor students were to be required to declare Anglican faith; the three benefactors were Catholic, Jewish and Nonconformist.

Despite opposition from the clerical establishment, and the foundation of rival King's College "preserving traditional

---

Street names along route 2A.2 and their origin

Byng
Georgiana Byng, daughter of Lord Torrington, was first wife of 6th Duke of Bedford
Endsleigh
Seat in Devon built by 6th Duke
Euston
Suffolk estate brought to Henry Fitzroy, Duke of Grafton, by his wife Isabella
Gower
Wife of 4th Duke of Bedford was daughter of Earl of Gower
Gordon
Wife of 6th Duke of Bedford was daughter of Duke of Gordon
Taviton
One of the estates in Devon given by Henry VIII to John Russell, first Earl of Bedford
Woburn
Principal seat of Dukes of Bedford

---

values" to the south, the foundation stone of UCL was laid on 30 April 1827 by the Duke of Sussex, the only son of George III who could be accused of having liberal leanings. The architect, selected after public competition, was William Wilkins, whose later National Gallery was much derided. As originally designed, the main block facing Gower Street was to have two projecting wings, but these materialised only later, and not to Wilkins' designs. His lodges were constructed, and still exist.

Building of the new university was distinctly fitful, and the imposing portico had nothing much behind it until the library was built there in 1849. The dome and much of the central block, including the library, were badly damaged in WW II and were afterwards restored by Sir Albert Richardson. In the 1990s the rotunda under the dome was restored, Flaxman's St Michael was brought into it out of the cold of the portico where it had languished for many years, and his sculpted plaques depicting various acts of charity which are set in the plaster of the wall were cleaned.

The present south wing, at right angles to Gower Street, was finally built in 1869-76 to house University College School (actually founded in 1830; it moved to Hampstead in 1907), and the north wing housing the Slade School of Fine Arts was built in 1871-81. By 1891 the south wing had made a 90° turn and was edging north again along Gower Street, some early 19th-century houses being demolished to make way for it. The new building housed the department of engineering.

The character of Gower Street changed

radically in 1892, when the university's rights over the roadway were bought by St Pancras Vestry for the colossal sum of £15,000 and the gates preserving it as a private road were removed (so that Miss Prism's reference, in *The Importance of Being Earnest* (1895), to the upsetting of a Gower Street omnibus "in younger, and happier, days" was an anachronism on the part of the immigrant Oscar Wilde).

Building for UCL continued apace in the early 20th century, with the Institute of Physiology on the old UCS playground in 1909, plus Pharmacology as a second stage in 1912, the School of Architecture facing Gower Street north of the main entrance in 1913, and a final extension yet further south along Gower Street in 1927 to accommodate Anatomy.

This spate of building was followed by a pause, the centre of development shifting in the 1930s to the Senate House site (p 62), but after WW II the inexorable march of the university down Gower Street continued, with the construction of the Biological Sciences building, which extends to Torrington Place, in 1964. Among the old buildings demolished to make way for it was No.104, once occupied by John Rylands, after whom the Rylands Library, Manchester is named; and No.100, occupied by Charles Darwin between 1838 and 1842 (blue plaque). On ground now covered by the Biological Sciences building, in what was then Upper Gower Street, Charles Dickens' mother tried in 1824 to open a school to help with the family finances. The school failed to attract any pupils, Dickens' father was imprisoned for debt and the 12-year-old Dickens was sent to work in a blacking factory. In 1985 the remaining gap on the east side of Gower Street was closed by a building of Sir Hugh Casson's.

Retracing our steps from Torrington Place (but remaining on the eastern pavement), we see on the west side of Gower Street several original houses that have survived, their Georgian plainness contrasting sharply with what came later. Millais is said to have lived at **No.87**; **No.99** housed *The Spectator* from the 1920s to 1975. At **No.91** a blue plaque commemorates George Dance the younger (1741-1825), an architect of immense influence in 18th- and 19th-century London, but also an artist and a founder member of the Royal Academy (see also p 66). **No.105**, housing the Royal National Institute for the Deaf since 1936, had a number of classical features added in the late 19th century. **No.111** is the university's Catholic chaplaincy, and **Nos.115-131** are student lodgings.

At the corner with University Street we see the Gower Street entrance to the UCL/UCH Medical School (p 41), this one with a confident classical portico setting off the colossal Ionic columns.

Go past UCL and turn right into **GOWER PLACE**, pausing on the corner to note, high up on the corner building (now the language school), the inscription **H K Lewis**. This was for decades *the* source of books (and skeletons) for UCL's medical students until it was absorbed as a department of Dillon's bookshop (p 64) down the road. In Gower Place we can admire the handsome classical façade of the building opened in 1913 as the university chemistry laboratories and named many years later after Kathleen Lonsdale, a pioneer crystallographer who in the 1920s first applied Fourier analysis to X-ray images from crystals to elucidate molecular structures; she was professor of chemistry at UCL 1946-68 and the first woman elected (1945) to the Royal Society. The building is now the Sandoz Institute for medical research, chemistry having moved round the corner into Gordon Street (next page).

Alongside there stands a red-brick building, containing the university's safety offices, in extravagant Flemish style, which the Department of National Heritage has listed "for its curiosity value". Further down on the opposite side is the red granite back of Unity House (p 50), whose entrance is at 205 Euston Road. No.44, long since demolished, was from 1827 to 1833 the home of William Godwin (p 18), political philosopher and widower of Mary Wollstonecraft (p 65). Much of the north-eastern end of the street is taken up by the back of the Wellcome Building, which fronts on the Euston Road (p 50).

At the eastern end of Gower Place turn right into **GORDON STREET**. The nine-storey red-brick Victorian building on the corner began life as the Endsleigh Palace Hotel, the upper front windows of which must have had a fair if oblique view of the Endsleigh Gardens which once stretched along the south side of enormous Euston Square all the way to Upper Woburn Place. The hotel was taken over during WW I as an officers' hospital. After the war the Seamen's Hospital, which originally operated from the Albert Dock Hospital (more appropriately than from Bloomsbury!), was enabled to buy and equip the building as a new Seamen's Hospital (p 46), on condition that it also housed the university's new School of Tropical Medicine. The School moved to Keppel Street (p 64) in 1929 but the Seamen's Hospital continued here until a landmine on 10 May 1941 made it untenable. It was acquired by UCL in 1959 and now houses its students' union.

Gordon Street was largely built by Thomas Cubitt, but none of his houses survive except **Nos.17 and 19**, which cower apologetically between later developments such as the above, and house the office of the college dean. The east side of the street is dominated by the uncompromising façade, characteristic of the brutalism fashionable in the 1960s and 1970s, of the Christopher Ingold chemistry laboratories, opened 1971 (Sir Christopher Ingold, FRS at 30, was one of the great English theoretical organic chemists of the early 20th century, and professor at UCL). Opposite looms the university's equally ugly Bloomsbury Theatre, built (1969, by James Cubitt [sic] and Partners) on the site of a university hall that was bombed in 1940. It had been opened in 1927 as part of the college's centenary celebrations, having been converted from All Saints' church (1846).

The last houses on the left as we pass down Gordon Street are in fact Nos.29-30 Gordon Square, with a modern façade in Regency style and containing the university department of Greek and Latin. On the corner of the Square stands a late-19th-century lamppost which retains its original carbon-arc fitting, the last remaining example in London of this type of lamp from the early days of electric street lighting.

We are now moving into the area developed from 1800 to the 1850s on the Bedford estate by, first, James Burton in 1800-1820 (most of whose surviving houses are to be seen in section 2B) and Thomas Cubitt in 1820-1850, with choice surviving examples in this section. Thomas Cubitt was the first building contractor to organise contracts as a whole, to employ all the builders and craftsmen directly and to have a central builders' yard from which all the materials were supplied - in the case of Bloomsbury, directly to the east, beyond Gray's Inn Road next to Cubitt Street, which he also built. After successfully developing Tavistock Square, Gordon Square and surrounding streets into a fashionable residential area he moved on to Hyde Park Gate, Pimlico and Belgravia, only too successfully competing with himself and making it very difficult to sell his later Gordon Square houses, as we shall see. He was assisted in all this by his younger brother Lewis, who designed King's Cross railway station and probably also many of the houses attributed to his more famous brother.

Our walk actually takes us backward in time: the side of Gordon Square built earliest is on the east. Keeping to the right down Gordon Street, the first house we encounter in **GORDON SQUARE** is No.26: Nos.27 and 28 have been demolished to make a back entrance into the main university campus. We continue down the west side (decreasing numbers), saving for a treat the range of Cubitt houses on the east. Those in this range, completed by Cubitt's executors after his death in 1855, are taller, more lavishly embellished, and altogether less successful.

Nos.16-26 are now university offices/classrooms, although formerly private houses. Sir Frederick Treves, befriender of the Elephant Man and remover of Edward VII's appendix

10 Picture taken during the construction of the Friends' House on the Euston Road in 1925. To the right, the Seamen's Hospital for Tropical Diseases. This moved into the Endsleigh Palace Hotel building after World War I. Straight ahead, the Endsleigh Hotel [sic], which was converted from a row of Cubitt houses forming part of the original south side of Euston Square, facing Endsleigh Gardens.

(a medical crisis which postponed his coronation) lived at **No.18**, 1880-4. **No.16** was built originally in 1848-9 in a florid Tudor style, toned down by a century's soot, as a student hall of residence. Its intrusion into a sober residential square reflects the financial desperation which both Cubitt and the Bedford Estate were experiencing when fashionable London was abandoning Bloomsbury for Hyde Park Gate or Belgravia and Cubitt's houses in Gordon Square were not being bought. Selling the leases of this large plot to the university and a much larger one to the south to the Irvingites (see below) came as welcome relief to the Bedford Office. Forty years later, No.14/15 was converted to house the library of the Rev. Dr Daniel Williams, who provided in his will (1729) for the establishment of a library of books relating to the Nonconformist movement. The Library had a series of homes before coming to rest here. A blue plaque commemorates Dr Robert Travers Herford, a Unitarian scholar and interpreter of Judaism.

At the south-west corner of the Square stands what is now the **University Church of Christ the King**. Looming over Bloomsbury like a beached whale, it was built 1851-4 for a charismatic sect known as the Irvingites, after its founder Edward Irving, a one-time Church of Scotland minister. They were noted for speaking in tongues and prophesying the millennium. The church itself, on a monumental scale, was never completed; only five of the projected seven bays of the nave were built, and a planned 300-ft spire, which would have challenged St Paul's itself, did not materialise. The church is now only partially visible amongst the surrounding buildings. Mainly Early English in style, with forays into Decorated, there are many beautiful internal details, a few of which may be glimpsed from the "English Chapel" at the east end beyond the high altar, which is the only part open to the public (as a meditation chapel), pending restoration of the main fabric, the entrance being from Gordon Square. The main entrance was from the north, through a set of cloisters, now closed.

At the corner of Gordon Square glance to the right and enjoy the view across **BYNG PLACE** to the building with a classical elevation. This was built by Cubitt in 1833, originally as three houses but soon converted (because they did not sell) into Coward College, which trained dissenting Protestant ministers. This was its fourth resting-place since being founded under the will of William Coward (died 1738). The college had moved to Swiss Cottage by 1850, where after amalgamation with others it became 'New College'. Since 1964 the building has been the International Centre for the Society of Friends. The building originally had stone balconies and other decoration.

Across Torrington Place once stood Nos.1-6 Gordon Square, now replaced by Charles Holden's competent but uninspired Warburg Institute (p 59), within which is installed the only part of No.1 salvaged from the demolition, a frieze depicting the nine muses (pp 48-9). We must lament the loss of the Cubitt block of houses, but rejoice that its mirror image **Nos.55-59** is still extant across what is simultaneously the south side of Gordon and the north side of Woburn Square - actually, an open space planted with shrubs and parked cars.

Thread your way along the narrow pavement immediately south of the Gordon Square garden, surely the most picturesque of London squares, awash with daffodils in the Spring and roses in the summer and crossed by winding paths, and pause at the southeast corner to take a closer look at **Nos.55-59**, which form a unit framed by broad stucco pilasters within a lively surface pattern. It contains a few parts of the university's Department of Education, most of which are housed in Lasdun's vast Institute of Education in Bedford Way (p 58), the side of which has obliterated No.54. **No.55** was once Miss Peters' private school for girls, and receives a mention in the diaries of Virginia Woolf: Clive and Vanessa Bell's children went there.

Across the road from these in **No.53**

Gordon Square (a superb Cubitt house, designed by him personally to re-house the owner of No.7 (on the opposite corner, displaced by the Irvingite church) is a very special museum: the Percival David Foundation, which displays the finest collection of Chinese ceramics outside China. The inscriptions on some of the porcelain have great historical significance. There is also a library of books related to Chinese art. Both were presented to the university in 1950 by Sir Percival David.

The east side of the Square is an unbroken range of Cubitt houses. Now almost entirely taken over by the university, it is rich in literary and other associations from the time when these were private houses. The blue plaque at **No.46**, recording the residence there of John Maynard Keynes from 1916 until his death in 1946, tells only half the story: it was to this house that the four children of Sir Leslie Stephen moved on the death of their father in 1904 and it was here that the Bloomsbury Group (p 13) was reconstituted from its Cambridge origins.

11   Side of No.1 Gordon Square, demolished 1955 to make way for the Warburg Institute (whose address is Woburn Square), showing the frieze of the nine muses in its wall. Opposite, the frieze (a Coade stone imitation of a Roman sarcophagus) now preserved inside the entrance of the Warburg Institute.

Vanessa Stephen continued to live here with her husband Clive Bell until 1916. Other noted inhabitants of this side of the Square included Kate O'Brien (novelist and playwright) at **No.37**, the artist Dora Carrington at **No.41**, the Oriental scholar Arthur Waley at **No.50** and Lytton Strachey and his mother at **No.51** (blue plaque). Between 1938 and 1956 **Nos.44-45** were home to the Orthological Institute founded by Charles Ogden, originator and promoter of Basic English. The occupation of **No.39** by the National Union of Women Teachers in 1922 marked the beginning of the conversion of this side of Gordon Square from residences to offices, and later to university use, a process virtually completed when Keynes' widow moved to Cambridge in 1948 - although one or two private residents are recorded as late as the 1950s.

After the architectural riches of the east side, the north side of the square is disappointing. Here a whole row of handsome Cubitt houses - the first to be built in this Square - was pulled down to make way for the university's Institute of Archaeology (founded 1937), **Nos.31-34**, a bland 6-storey building opened in 1958, which also until recently sheltered the Institute of Classical Studies founded shortly before. The eastern part of the building is the side of the examination halls in Taviton Street, which intrude on the Square where No.35 used to be.

The north-east corner of Gordon Square forms a junction with Taviton Street and Endsleigh Place. **ENDSLEIGH PLACE** remains today almost wholly as Cubitt built it, and it is worth pausing to enjoy the beauty of what is essentially a street linking two squares. On the north, linking the ends of Taviton and Endsleigh Streets, the row of Cubitt houses is now Passfield Hall, a university hall of residence. On the south we see Cubitt's elegant return frontages of 36 Gordon Square and of 29 Tavistock Square, the former housing the Association of Commonwealth Universities and the latter the Committee of Vice-Chancellors and Principals of UK universities.

Returning to **TAVITON STREET**, we note the pretty frieze on the east wall of Passfield Hall (there is a twin on the west wall). Most of the west side has been sacrificed to the university's modern examination halls and only **Nos.20-24** survive, somewhat plainer than the usual Cubitt style (probably completed by his executors after his death). The handsome east side, however, has survived almost complete. A blue plaque on **Nos.5-10** (converted to another hall of residence)

commemorates the Rev. Hugh Price Hughes (1847-1902), a Methodist preacher.

At the top of Taviton Street, on the east side facing Endsleigh Gardens, stands Wates House, home to the university's Environmental Studies department. It was funded largely by a grant from the Wates Foundation and opened in 1975. A harmonious, pleasing design, the frontage is not significantly marred by three curious little porticoes which serve no evident functional purpose.

Turning right into **ENDSLEIGH GARDENS**, we see a row of Cubitt houses, originally the south side of Euston Square, which he developed under an 1829 contract with the Southampton Estate, owner of the land here on both sides of the New Road. He had already completed much of the east side of this Square, now of course obliterated. The houses boast substantial porticoes with Doric columns and balconies above. Opposite is the back of the Friends' Meeting House, and we need now to make a short detour into the **EUSTON ROAD**.

Passing through the charming Friends' garden (open to the public, and you can picnic there if you wish, but no alcohol!) and turning left, we face the front of the Meeting House. The ground on which it stands, as well as the ground to the east as far as Upper Woburn Place, was once part of the gardens of Euston Square. When in

the 1920s the leases of the houses, which had access to the gardens, began to fall in they were bought by Sir Alfred Butt, a theatrical impresario and property developer, who made it a condition of resale that the purchasers should have no rights over the gardens, so he could be free to build on them. Despite protests the eastern part was sold to various developers, including the GPO and LCC - until 1990 there was a fire station facing down Endsleigh Street - and the western part to the Society of Friends, who were outgrowing their headquarters in Houndsditch. The design of the new meeting house, the competition for which was confined to Quaker architects, was won by Hubert Lidbetter. His plain but dignified design, with stately Doric columns, won the 1926 RIBA award for best building of the year.

The refusal of St Pancras Council to intervene to preserve an open space here caused an outcry and the setting up of a Royal Commission on London Squares, and in due course the LCC acquired statutory powers to veto any such developments in future.

Continuing along the Euston Road past Drayton House (a continuation of the Friends' House, but let out as offices) and crossing Gordon Street we come to the **Wellcome Building**. Built in 1931-2 by Septimus Warwick to house the laboratories and collection of medically

related objects of Sir Henry Wellcome (1853-1936), co-founder of the pharmaceutical company, it was between 1947 and 1989 the headquarters of the company (confusingly called the Wellcome Foundation), which is now located further east and across the Euston Road. In 1986 it became the headquarters of the Wellcome Trust (the medical charity into which all the profits of the company are poured), of the Wellcome Institute for the History of Medicine and of several smaller medical charities within the building. The emphatic Ionic columns (typical of the 1930s) on the elegant classical façade are in marked contrast to the restrained Doric of the Friends' House. The interior space is also very grand. The buildings between here and the corner of Gower Street are unremarkable office blocks, apart from Unity House, home of the National Union of Rail, Maritime and Transport Workers.

Retracing our steps, we pass back through the Friends' garden and into **ENDSLEIGH STREET**. Note the carved reliefs of soldiers and workers set into the upper floor of Bentham House (once a trade union building), an otherwise unassuming art deco construction housing the university law faculty. In a house on

12 West side of Tavistock Square (Cubitt, 1830). In the foreground, the memorial to conscientious objectors (see p 52).

this site lived for a time William Michael Rossetti (1829-1919), brother of the better-known Dante Gabriel, a noted art critic and man of letters and a member of the Pre-Raphaelite Brotherhood, together with his sister Christina (p 60). Next comes B'nai B'rith House, HQ of a Jewish charity: a good modern design, yet out of place amongst the Cubitt houses. A move to demolish **Nos.3-4** to build the headquarters of the National Union of Students was thwarted by the Department of the Environment in 1971, which is why the HQ is in Malet Street instead. Arthur Waley, whom we have already met in Gordon Square, lived for a time at **No.36**.

As late as 1893 Endsleigh Street was the site of one of the gates that used to close off the Bedford estate from the north (see also p 39). These impediments to traffic, which were particularly resented so close to three main-line railway termini, were finally banished by the London Streets (Removal of Gates) Acts of 1890 and 1893.

At the corner of Endsleigh Street and **TAVISTOCK SQUARE** stands Tavistock Court, built 1934-5 as its headquarters by the National Free Church Council, which amalgamated with the Federal Council of Evangelical Free Churches to become the Free Churches Federal Council in 1940. Much of the building is also rented out as flats. Two of the reliefs on the façade seem to depict the story of St Hubert: a stag with a crucifix between its antlers was seen by a huntin' nobleman who thereafter turned religious, eventually becoming Bishop of Liège. The reason for this choice of subject seems to have died with the architect.

Only the west side of Tavistock Square has survived the ravages of World War II and redevelopment, and even here only the façade is intact. It is the earliest (1825-6) and perhaps the handsomest of the surviving Cubitt ranges hereabouts (Fig 12, p 51). Summerson speculates that these houses may have been designed by younger brother Lewis rather than Thomas Cubitt, who certainly built them to a high standard. Thomas Beale (1886-1945), novelist of the East End and author of *Living in Bloomsbury* lived at **No.33** in the 1930s, where there is a brown Camden Council plaque to Mohammed Ali Abbas (1922-1979), who worked tirelessly for the creation of a separate state of Pakistan, and presided here over a kind of informal Pakistani embassy before the state was formed.

In contrast to Gordon Square, the gardens of Tavistock Square are rigidly formal. In the northwest corner is a large memorial stone dedicated to conscientious objectors, which was unveiled in June 1994 by Sir Michael Tippett as a calculated response to the D-Day celebrations. At the Centre, for no known reason, is a fine statue of Mahatma Gandhi by the Polish-born Fredda Brilliant. It was unveiled by Prime Minister Harold Wilson on 17 May 1968, the cost of £10,000 being met by public subscription. A move in the 1980s to rename the square Gandhi Square came to nothing. In the southeast corner stands the double bust of Dame Louisa Brandreth Aldrich-Blake (1865-1925), who was one of the first women surgeons in this country and dean of the Royal Free Hospital School of Medicine for Women from 1914 to 1925. The plinth and stone seat below it were designed by Lutyens.

The south side of the square is now occupied by the Tavistock Hotel, which contains some amusing art deco interiors. One of the houses which the hotel superseded, No.52, was the home of Leonard and Virginia Woolf 1924-1939; the Hogarth Press was in the basement and Virginia wrote many of her best-known works there. Most of these houses were destroyed by bombing in WW II.

The east side of the square was originally developed by James Burton in 1803, and his houses survived until 1938. After WW II they were replaced by tall office blocks in red brick. Further north, at the end of a drive which continued the line of the north side of the Square, Burton built a grand house for himself, Tavistock House, where he lived 1801-6. This faced north, with the garden front facing extensive grounds stretching to Tavistock Place. The house was later divided into no fewer than three grand houses, one of which was the last, and largest, of Charles Dickens' London houses, 1851-60. The whole was demolished in 1901; the lease of the site was sold to the Theosophical Society in 1912 and Lutyens was engaged to design for it a combined headquarters and college. Work began in 1914, but WW I intervened and the completed half of the building was acquired by the War Office. Offered to the Society of Friends (p 50) in 1920, it was eventually taken over by the British Medical Association and completed in 1929. The main frontage, in "monumental classical style" (National Heritage), is certainly imposing; the low frontages on either side were intended to harmonise with Burton's houses flanking them, and now seem incongruous.

To our left, on the corner of the square with Upper Woburn Place, stands Woburn House, until 1995 the home of the Jewish Museum and Court of the Chief Rabbi. The museum moved to Albert Street, Camden Town in May of that year. The house seems destined to be offices.

Partway up Upper Woburn Place, on the right, is pedestrianised and charming **WOBURN WALK**, a Regency gem built by Cubitt in 1822 as a street of bow-windowed shops (almost the first planned shopping precinct!), and restored to its original purpose from a fairly parlous state by St Pancras Borough Council in 1959. In 1974 it won the Cleary prize for the best shopping street in London. The plaque on **No.5** (not, curiously, a blue one) records the fact that W B Yeats lived there for 25 years from 1895 (when the poet was 30) to 1919; during this period it was in effect the London headquarters of the Anglo-Irish literary set. The building, together with its neighbours, is now part of the New Ambassadors hotel. Opposite at **No.2** lived for a time the novelist Dorothy Richardson, and at **No.18** the 19th-century radical orator and founding father of the cooperative movement, George Holyoake.

UPPER WOBURN PLACE is given over largely to hotels and apartment buildings of varying architectural quality. The utterly plain façade of Endsleigh Court and the County Hotel depress the

13 Woburn Lodge, built by the Inwoods (p 54) as their residence in the 1820s, demolished 1930.

spirits. The Ambassadors Hotel (an older building dating from the early 1900s but completely refurbished in the 1960s) incongruously sports a baroque pediment surmounting a square modern entrance canopy. Beyond it we are slightly cheered by the honest classicism of Century House, a 1930s office block built on the site of a much-loved 1820s building known as Woburn Lodge (previous page) which was demolished in 1930. Opposite stands the last survivor of Cubitt's development, the Euston Plaza (formerly Cora) Hotel. Its confident Corinthian pilasters (in the so-called Tivoli order), well integrated into both front and side elevations, put to shame the mixed and muddled 20th-century efforts surrounding it. During WW II it housed a Liberty Club for US servicemen.

Finally we come to St Pancras New Church, which was built 1819-1822 on Lord Southampton's estate to cater for the growing population of a neighbourhood which could no longer be accommodated in the medieval St Pancras church in Pancras Road. The architects were William Inwood and his son Henry (see Fig 13, p 53), and the design was based, with what was considered scrupulous attention to classical detail, on parts of the Erechtheum at Athens. Henry Inwood visited Athens - no light undertaking in those days - in order to make drawings of both the Erechtheum and the Tower of the Winds, renderings of which in two sizes form the two lowest stages of the steeple. This is finally surmounted by a cross instead of a Triton weathervane, in a belated affirmation that this is a Christian church, not a pagan temple. The two curious wings flanking the apse at the east end are mirror-image versions of the south porch of the Erechtheum, but with four instead of six caryatids each. They are of Coade stone on cast-iron bases and Rossi, the sculptor, has succeeded in making them look more Roman than Greek. They carry ewers and inverted torches, the latter being symbols of death, appropriately enough as the wings give access to the burial vaults. The church was consecrated by the Bishop of London on 7 May 1822, and Summerson considered it "the parish church *par excellence* of Regency England" - though some contemporaries considered it improper to use a pagan temple as the basis for a Christian church. Damaged during WW II, it was extensively restored in 1951-2.

From St Pancras New Church a short walk across Euston Road and the remains of Euston Square Gardens brings us to Euston main line and Underground stations.

From Russell Square to Senate House

The massive picturesque walk starts from the Russell Square Underground station. The station is actually some 50 yards from the north-east corner of the Square, in Bernard Street. Walk westwards from the station to the Square, the largest in London except for Lincoln's Inn Fields, and take in the massive, picturesque frontage of the Russell Hotel on your left.

All street names in this section are derived from members of the Bedford family, whose family name is Russell, or from estates belonging to them, their wives or wives' relations, with only four exceptions, which we shall encounter around Store Street at the western edge of the section.

The Russell Hotel is a comparatively late arrival on the **RUSSELL SQUARE** scene. The first house on this site was built in 1763 and successively inhabited by Lord Baltimore, the Duke of Bolton and Lord Loughborough. This house was demolished when Burton built the east side of Russell Square, between 1800 and 1817. The hotel, dated 1898 over the main entrance, was designed by the Bedford estates' architect, Charles Fitzroy Doll, in flamboyant "super-François Premier style, magnificently inflated to eight storeys" (Pevsner). Four full-length female figures in costumes of different periods stand above and to the left and right of the main

---

Street names along route 2B.1 and their origin

Montague
1st duke of Montagu married stepsister of Lady Rachel Russell

Russell
Family name of the dukes (at first, earls) of Bedford

Thornhaugh
Estate brought into the Russell family by the marriage of Anne Sapcote to John Russell, 1st earl

Torrington
Father-in-law of 6th duke

Woburn
Principal seat of the dukes of Bedford

---

entrance. They probably are meant to represent the four Protestant English queens Elizabeth, Mary II, Anne and Victoria - although the last does not have the comfortable figure of contemporary portraits. In a frieze below the balcony floor are coats of arms of various European royal and noble families (in the hope they would patronise the hotel?).

Russell Square was developed by Burton at the behest of the 5th Duke of Bedford after 1800: first the east and then the south side, and, while Humphrey Repton was laying out the gardens, the west and part of the north side. The Russell Hotel occupies the sites of Nos.1-9 (numbering began, curiously, at Guilford Street and went anticlockwise as well as antihistorically).

No.5, long displaced by the Russell Hotel, once (1856) housed F D Maurice, founder of Christian Socialism and Working Men's Colleges; No.8 housed Sylvia Pankhurst and her daughter Christabel in the 1880s. Surprisingly, Edgar Allan Poe (1809-49) was another who spent five of his early years (1815-1820) in Russell Square.

Proceeding south past the Russell Hotel we cross Guilford Street and see, set in the pavement at the corner, a sort of memorial to the Turkish baths which used to grace the basement of the old Imperial Hotel, also built by Doll (1907-1911) in an even more extravagant style than the Russell. This was replaced in the 1960s by a smaller, modern Imperial Hotel and the President Hotel, both of which doubtless have more up-to-date facilities, but hardly merit a passing glance. The ground floor of both is let out to banks and shops to increase the rent revenue.

It is ironic to think, as the tour buses hurtle past with their stench of diesel fuel, that the poet Thomas Gray (1716-1771) took lodgings in a cottage here in order to enjoy the pure air and the clear view northwards to Hampstead. The dashing portraitist Lawrence chose to live in one of Burton's houses here (No.65) in 1820 when he was finishing the portraits of the Allies triumphant in the Napoleonic Wars which hang in the Waterloo Room at Windsor Castle. Legend has it that when the Russian general Platoff was sitting for him, the house was guarded by Cossacks mounted on white chargers. Later residents included Mrs Humphry Ward at No.61 and Richard D'Oyly Carte at No.71.

Dodging the traffic aiming for Southampton Row (p 79), we cross to the surviving Burton houses (early 1800s), Nos.60-52; they acquired terracotta ornaments in 1899. The impressive dimensions of these houses can sometimes be glimpsed when the interior of the ground floor is being remodelled and one can see through to the mature trees in the gardens beyond. In one such house, **No.58**, lived George Grossmith (1847-1912), co-author of *Diary of a Nobody* and entertainer, while his brother Weedon lived at 1 Bedford Square.

Across **BEDFORD PLACE**, a modern office block has replaced Nos. 50-51, where the architect G E Street (1824-1881) once lived. Despite their plain uniformity, the houses of Bedford Place were very popular when they were first built, during a building slump occasioned by the Napoleonic wars; remarkably, the frontages survived WW II bombing and form a pleasing, if unexciting, ensemble. They have now almost without exception become small hotels. In 1800 Edward Jenner occupied **No.15** for a year while introducing smallpox vaccination to London (Fig 14) at the Bloomsbury Dispensary (p 76) in Great Russell Street. T S Eliot also lived for a year (1914-15) in Bedford Place - at **No.28**. The dramatist Richard Cumberland (1732-1811), caricatured as Sir Fretful Plagiary in Sheridan's *The Critic*, died at **No.30**.

From the corner of Bedford Place we have a good view of Sir Richard Westmacott's statue on a high plinth of the 5th Duke of Bedford (1765-1802), erected posthumously in 1809 and covered with ornaments (plough, gifts of Ceres) reflecting his agricultural interests. He it was who pulled down Bedford House in what is now Bloomsbury Square (p 80) and started all this building.

Moving on around the Square, we encounter Montague Street (p 76), originally the boundary between the grounds of Southampton/Bedford House and those of Montagu House, and then some unadorned original Burton houses (Nos.43-38) on the west side of the Square, backing onto the grounds of the British Museum. These appear to be continuous with the houses of Montague Street, but a closer look reveals significant differences in fenestration and architraves.

Nos.40-38 (entrance to the latter in Montague Place) house research laboratories of the British Museum.

MONTAGUE PLACE is dominated on the south by the Edward VII Galleries of the British Museum, commissioned in 1905 and built by Sir John Burnet to the north of Smirke's original North wing (1833-8). Pevsner says they are in the chastest Beaux Arts style, "a very successful example of Classical Re-Revival". They were opened in 1914 by King George V, after his father's death. The north side is occupied by 1930s buildings, outposts of Senate House, and the side of **Stewart House**, built in the 1980s to replace Nos.37-31 Russell Square, with a pleasing façade imitating Burton's houses at Nos.38-43. At the entrance to Senate House's car park looms **No.30 Russell Square** (note the *art nouveau* lettering), a heavy 1913-14 construction by Sir John Burnet built to house the Royal Institute of Chemistry (and still so labelled), which has since merged with the Chemical Society to form the Royal Society of Chemistry, now grandly housed at Burlington House, Piccadilly. Notice over the entrance the thoughtful, seated figure of the father of

14 Cartoon by Gillray illustrating common fears of possible outcomes of Edward Jenner's inoculation with cowpox vaccine, which he introduced in London in 1800.

57

British chemistry, Joseph Priestley, with his dates (1733-1804). The building replaced the one in which Henry Crabb Robinson, one of the founders of University College London, lived from 1839 to 1867.

Then come some more terrace houses, Nos.29-25, all except No.29 heavily restored and now occupied by university departments. Lurking at the corner is the side of a 1995 building, aligned with the Burton architecture as to skyline and fenestration but unfortunately in bricks the colours of hot desert sands: the Brunei Gallery, built to house examples of Islamic art. The University of London has grudgingly placed on it a small grey plaque recording its "sincere apologies that the plans of this building were settled without due consultation with the Russell family and their Trustees and hence without their approval of its design". No comment.

The gap in the northwest corner of the Square is all that remains of **THORNHAUGH STREET** - see the label on the side wall of **No.24** Russell Square, which also bears a bronze plaque recording the fact that T S Eliot worked here 1925-1965 as a director of Faber & Faber. On Wyld's 1828 map this is called Upper Montague Street. It leads to the pitiful remains of Woburn Square, to which we return anon.

The north side of Russell Square contains, first, a few more remaining Burton houses (Nos.24-21), with terracotta ornament added later, where we may imagine either the Sedleys or the Osbornes in *Vanity Fair* residing (Thackeray's numbers 62 and 96 were fictitious: although 62 existed, 96 did not). There is a bronze plaque on **No.21** naming Sir Samuel Romilly (1757-1818) (Fig 15), law reformer and pioneer of abolition of slavery, who moved here from 48 Gower Street (p 65) in 1803, taking the first 99-year lease on the newly built house. He committed suicide here in 1818, unable to bear the death of his wife.

Nos.19-17 were demolished to make room for the university's Institute of Education (also containing University Hall and part of the Law Department) by Lasdun (1971-6), which occupies the whole of the west side of Bedford Way (formerly Upper Bedford Place), with westward extensions, see later. The final stretch of the north side of the Square, from Bedford Way to Woburn Place, is occupied by a singularly neutral building with three pillared porches, labelled on the eastern side **Russell Square House**.

This building has an unexpectedly interesting history. The eastern half was finished in 1941, having been intended as an extension of the Royal National Hotel (this page). It was used first as a hostel for US servicemen, then as headquarters for the Ministry of Information, before the latter moved into Senate House. When the Paymaster General's Office moved in in 1947 the western wall was still blank, but by 1952 the western half had been built to match the eastern half exactly. The join is invisible except to the eagle-eyed. The lease on the western half was taken in 1955 by the Ministry of Health, which became the DHSS and later the Department of Health; it remained the occupier until 1996. Interestingly, Health began to displace the PGO (to 1-6 Tavistock Square, p 52) in 1957 and by the 1980s occupied both halves of the building (easily done because of the identical construction and the existence of continuous internal corridors), only to withdraw again to Nos.13-16 in favour of a firm of management and financial advisers at Nos.10-12, and vacated altogether in 1995. The basement of the Health building used to contain physics laboratories in which new types of equipment and hospital instruments were tested. Very recently (1997) this western half of the building has been refaced, and gained a plaque commemorating Sir George Williams (1821-1905), founder of the Young Men's Christian Association, who lived at No.13 (when these were separate Burton houses) from 1879 until his death.

There is no remaining trace of the early 19th century in either **WOBURN PLACE** or **BEDFORD WAY,** long stretches of both streets being occupied by the Royal National Hotel, a barrack-like 84-bay building devoid of distinction, though less

arrogant than the Institute of Education opposite. Both lead to the south side of Tavistock Square occupied by the modern Tavistock Hotel. The original Bedford Way, or rather Upper Bedford Place, was completed (by John McGill) only in the 1820s, after the first building spurt that produced Bedford Place (p 56) in 1801-6 had sputtered and died.

With a glance at Cubitt's strong and distinguished west side of Tavistock Square (p 51), we walk west for 50 yards and turn south into the sad remnants of **WOBURN SQUARE**. This, like Torrington Square, was never square but a long narrow rectangle. Some of the original buildings have been adapted into university offices; most have been destroyed, to make way for the entrances to yet more car parks as well as the Warburg Institute (on the northwest corner), a functional building (1958) designed by Charles Holden, architect of Senate House, which replaced Nos.1-6 Gordon Square. Its neighbour to the south, which housed the Courtauld Collection of paintings until the latter moved to Somerset House in 1989/90, is now a Study Centre for the Slade School of Fine Art. It is ironic that two institutions devoted to the study and appreciation of art should present so inartistic an appearance. Immediately inside the Warburg Institute is preserved the frieze depicting the nine muses which formerly

15 *Sir Samuel Romilly (1757-1818), who lived and died at 21 Russell Square.*

graced the side elevation of No.1 Gordon Square (p 48).

In the middle of the east side of Woburn Square, after the surviving **Nos.18-10** (with good balcony railings) there formerly stood a grand church, Christ Church, visible in the 1963 aerial photograph on p 2 and on p 62, which was built by Lewis Vulliamy in 1831-3 as a chapel of ease to St George's, Bloomsbury (p 75) when the population of Bloomsbury was at its height. Burne-Jones added stained glass to the church, but it was demolished in 1974 - admittedly when it had fallen into a poor state of repair and was no longer needed by the dwindling local population - to make way for the Institute of Education (with three stepped extensions into Woburn Square) as well as an extension to the School of Oriental and African Studies (SOAS). Note in passing that **No.15** retains its torch snuffer by the entrance.

Make your way southwards towards SOAS's main building (the acronym is displayed down its edge), which displaced the whole south side of the Square. Turn right, and noting neat **Nos.28-24** in the west side (like those on the east, all occupied by university departments), pass through the wide gap into the remains of **TORRINGTON SQUARE**, of which only a range on the east, Nos.27-32, survives. This Square was constructed earlier (1821-5) than Woburn Square (1829), in both cases by a family of builders by the name of Sim (James, James Jr and Robert) working to elevations required by the Bedford estate. In the 1790s this land had been rented by the Toxophilite Society, but it was given up in 1805 as houses sprang up around.

The actor and actor-manager Charles Kean (1811-68), son of the more famous Edmund, lived at **No.3** while managing the Princess's Theatre in Oxford Street, where he pioneered the use of limelight. Christina Rossetti (1830-1894) lived at **No.30** from 1876 until her death (bronze plaque, c.1913, to the 'poetess'), largely as an invalid but continuing to produce many of her most celebrated poems.

By the middle of the 19th century the mews courtyards around this area and Keppel Street (which then ran from Gower Street to Russell Square through where Senate House now stands) were turning into not very well-kept livery stables where germs flourished. Clearance of these mews areas eventually liberated land for the construction of Senate House in the 1930s.

Return through Thornhaugh Street to Russell Square, where you can either re-embark on the Underground or one of the buses passing through to the north or south; or proceed to route 2B.2.

From Senate House to Goodge Street station

From Russell Square we approach Senate House via a small car park, doubtless deemed adequate in the 1930s. Charles Holden's towering building, or complex of buildings, has had (as one might expect) a mixed reception. Contemporary opinion on its completion in 1937 was almost universally favourable, indeed enthusiastic, perhaps because it was thought to be merely the first phase of a grandiose range of buildings stretching north all the way to Torrington Place (p 62).

The *Manchester Guardian* compared Holden to Wren and Barry, while the *Daily Sketch* opined that modern architecture in concrete had seldom achieved anything more outstanding. More critical views came to be voiced later. Pevsner compared it unfavourably with the architect's Underground stations, whilst more robust verdicts came from Evelyn Waugh ("grim mass of masonry") and Max Beerbohm ("bleak, bland, and hideous"). It formed the model for the Ministry of Truth in George Orwell's *1984*; many writers worked there in the Ministry of Information in World War II (WW II). It is said that Hitler ordered his bombers to spare it as he fancied it for his head-quarters in London.

The university's plans for a purpose-built main building in Bloomsbury go back to before WW I, when Lutyens prepared a design embodying an open court opposite the new King Edward VII Galleries at the north entrance to the British Museum, to be surrounded by buildings on the New Delhi scale and flanked by two large towers. The war interrupted these plans, and when they were revived in the 1920s they were for a colossal spinal building stretching from Montague Place to Torrington Place which would have wiped out Torrington Square altogether. Despite George V's dour observation that the design looked like a battleship it aroused much enthusiasm, and the few who pointed to the vandalism of destroying one of London's open spaces were little heeded. It was primarily shortage of funds which in the end compelled a more modest approach, if 'modest' can be used of the present building.

A site between Montague Place, Torrington Place, Malet Street and Russell and Woburn Squares had been partially cleared before the war, when Keppel Street and its associated Mews were being demolished (p 60) in preparation for a redevelopment which was slow to take place. The houses erected here on the Bedford estate by less scrupulous builders than Burton and Cubitt were so poorly built that by the time their 99-year leases fell in they had no value. After many years of political in-fighting, the Keppel Street sites were added to the parcel of land bought in 1927 from the Bedford estate with the aid of a grant from the ever-generous Rockefeller Foundation, and parliamentary powers to alter the road layout were obtained the following year. There were more delays while the required funds were amassed, but the foundation stone was finally laid by King George V and Queen Mary in June 1933 and the building was formally opened in 1936.

There were plans for a large university hall fronting Russell Square, and a row of Burton houses was demolished to make way for it, but WW II intervened and the hall was never built. For this we must be thankful: the proposal was for a huge slab-sided building which would have been a major eyesore, whereas the present modest Stewart House neatly imitates the rest of the west side of the Square.

Continuing across our car park we cross the dignified vestibule of Senate House and so across another car park into **MALET STREET**, which was created in 1906/7, on the initiative of the Bedford estate. However, none of the present buildings predate WW I. Turning right, we see a mixed range of inter-war buildings across the way, and self-consciously post-WW II buildings on the east side. Of the latter there are three: the two halves of Birkbeck

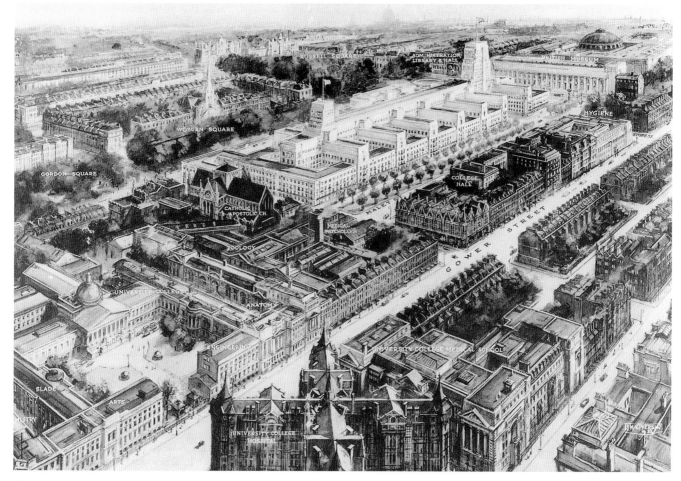

GORDON SQUARE · WOBURN SQUARE · RUSSELL SQUARE · ADMINISTRATION LIBRARY & HALL · BRITISH MUSEUM · HYGIENE · STORE ST · CATHOLIC APOSTOLIC CH. · COLLEGE HALL · MEDICAL PSYCHOLOGY · MALET · GOWER STREET · ZOOLOGY · UNIVERSITY COLLEGE · ANATOMY · UNIVERSITY COLLEGE MEDICAL SCHOOL · ENGINEERING · SLADE · ARTS · CHEMISTRY · UNIVERSITY COLLEGE HOSPITAL · J.W. ALBERY

62

College, started before WW II and completed in 1951, and the university Student's Union, opened in 1955, all by Charles Holden. On the west side we see, first the side of the London School of Hygiene and Tropical Medicine (p 65), then the back of No.52 Gower Street (dated 1924, quite late for this particular brand of 'Pont Street Dutch'), then the Vanbrugh theatre, showcase for RADA students. This is a post-WW II rebuilding, the original theatre having been destroyed by bombing; note the original foundation stone dated 1913 and inscribed with a roll-call of the pre-WW I theatrical establishment. Then comes the College Hall, built in the 1930s as a hall of residence for female students who had outgrown their first home in former Coward College (p 47). During WW II this building served as a hostel for overseas servicemen, and was badly damaged by bombing.

Passing Dilke House (1930s classical, housing several offices) we turn left into **TORRINGTON PLACE**. Nowadays its fame rests on the presence of Dillon's university bookshop, whose architectural splendours we now encounter. Built in 1908 as a cooperative venture between

16 *Original design for Senate House and associated buildings (Illustrated London News, 21 January 1933).*

Street names along route 2B.2 and their origins

Alfred
Christian name of builder of Alfred Place
Chenies
Estate with manor house in Bucks. brought into the Russell family by marriage
Gower
Wife of 4th Duke of Bedford was daughter of Earl of Gower
Huntley
Second wife of 6th Duke of Bedford was granddaughter of Marquess of Huntly
Keppel
Elizabeth Keppel was sister-in-law to the 4th duke and mother of the 5th and 6th dukes
Ridgmount
Estate in Bedfordshire purchased by 2nd duke

Russell
Family name of the dukes of Bedford
Malet
Sir Edward Malet, son-in-law of the 9th duke, one-time British ambassador in Berlin
Montague
1st Duke of Montagu married stepsister of Lady Rachel Russell
Thornhaugh
Like Chenies
Store
Unknown
Torrington
Father-in-law of 6th duke
Woburn
Principal seat of the dukes of Bedford

private developers and the university, which owned the site, this building at first housed several shops. Designed by Charles Fitzroy Doll, its kinship with the flamboyant Russell Hotel (p 55) is immediately apparent. Described by the Department of National Heritage, with some restraint, as in "elaborate Franco-Flemish-Gothic style", its gabled skyline and sweeping decoration offer a complete contrast to the London School of Hygiene and Tropical Medicine at the southern end of the same block. By so much did

architectural tastes change from the Edwardian to the post-war years (pp 64, 65). Across Gower Street from the side of Dillon's, the western range (**Nos.85 to 15A**) of Gower Street right down to Chenies Street is designed as a 'palace frontage', with the central houses built higher than their neighbours and the end houses jutting forward; the doorcases too are grander than the range either north or south of here. Most of these houses have been converted into small hotels. On the east side below Dillon's, three nice fanlights survive (Nos.80-74), then comes a modern building, No.66-72, housing several UCL departments and a Health Authority building. On the pilastered frontage of **No.52**, Bonham-Carter House, is an Association of Anaesthetists plaque stating that the first anaesthetic (ether) in England was given in a house on this site on 19 December 1846. Robert Liston, professor of surgery at UCH, was to give the first *public* demonstration of an operation under anaesthetic at the hospital up the road a few days later.

Then comes the side of the London School of Hygiene and Tropical Medicine, whose main entrance is in **KEPPEL STREET**, into which we now turn. Over the entrance is a frieze depicting what appears at first sight to be an Assyrian chariot, but is in fact intended to depict Aesculapius, Greek god of healing. In the ironwork, recently regilded, are

disease-carrying creatures (rat, flea, mosquito). Before the School was built in 1926-8, the site had long been cleared of the poor-quality early 19th-century houses put up here in defiance of the standards laid down by the Bedford estate. Before WW I it was hoped that a national theatre would rise on this site: a cluster of mock-Tudor buildings was constructed here in which Shakespeare was played and which during the war provided a club (known as the 'Shakespeare hut') for servicemen in

transit. After the war, on land bought for the university with the aid of the Rockefeller Foundation, was erected the present confident white building (opened 1930) on which, between the laurel wreaths more or less *de rigueur* on public edifices at the time, appear the names of such pioneers of microbiology and public health as Pasteur, Koch, Jenner and Lister.

Keppel Street originally ran right through to Russell Square. At No.16, where Senate House now stands, the novelist Anthony Trollope was born (much of the action of *Lady Anna* takes place in Keppel Street and nearby Bedford Square). Dickens' father died in Keppel Street, after an operation unassisted by anaesthesia.

At the southeast corner with Malet Street note the boundary stones (St Giles/St George's Bloomsbury) fixed into the wall. Turn right, down the rump of Malet Street, circling the fine sunken university garden into which the back gardens of Nos.2-20 Gower Street open and where one can imagine Lady Ottoline Morrell at No.10 holding garden parties

17, 18 Contrasting buildings at either end of a block in Gower Street: (left) the row of shops (1908) by Doll on the corner of Torrington Place, now occupied in its entirety by Dillon's bookshop, and (right) the London School of Hygiene and Tropical Medicine (1926) at Keppel Street.

(1924-1930). The ground is sunken, possibly (but this is pure speculation) because the brickearth here was of particularly good quality, deeply dug out for use in local building. Turning right again along a bit of Montague Place takes us to the corner of Bedford Square (p 70) and the bottom of Gower Street. The house on this corner, which is actually No.11 Bedford Square (p 71), carries a plaque to Henry Cavendish (1731-1810), discoverer of hydrogen and the molecular composition of water. He performed all his experiments in this house, not in the famous physics laboratory in Cambridge subsequently named after him, which houses many of his instruments.

North of this house, **No.2 GOWER STREET** bears a blue plaque to Dame Millicent Garrett Fawcett (1847-1929), a campaigner for women's suffrage, a founder of Newnham College, Cambridge and sister of Elizabeth Garrett Anderson, the first woman doctor in England; the hospital named after the latter lies just north of Bloomsbury. Millicent's husband was Henry Fawcett MP (1833-1884), who though blinded young in a shooting accident became (1863) professor of political economy at Cambridge and was elected Liberal MP in 1865. As Postmaster-General he invented postal orders, parcel post, sixpenny telegrams, savings stamps and the little number on pillarboxes which advertises the time of the next collection. He strongly supported his wife's political activities, although he did not live to see their successful outcome.

Luke Hansard (1752-1858), printer to the House of Commons and now remembered as the name on the (supposedly) verbatim reports from that Chamber, lived at **No.4** from 1808 to 1810. On **No.10** is a blue plaque to Lady Ottoline Morrell, society hostess, patron and sometime lover of several Bloomsbury and other writers ranging from D H Lawrence (*Women in Love*) through Aldous Huxley (*Crome Yellow*) to Bertrand Russell. Her main abode

was Garsington Manor near Oxford until 1924, then this house until about 1935. At **No.14** Sarah Siddons lived 1784-9, but the blue plaque here commemorates James Robinson (1813-1862), pioneer of anaesthesia and dentistry, who was presumably the doctor who administered the first anaesthetic at No.52 up the road, as recorded by the plaque there.

Across the road, between Nos.7 and 9, opens the surprisingly peaceful **GOWER MEWS**, parallel not to Gower Street but to the north side of Bedford Square, whose coach houses have been replaced by the row of garages with rooms above that you see on the left. On the right are the minuscule flats called Gower Mews Mansions. High above the far end of the Mews you can see the fabric canopy of Imagination House in Store Street.

Just beyond Gower Mews, as we retrace our steps up Gower Street, **STORE STREET** (origin of the name unknown) opens up on our left. There is nothing today to tell us that we are now leaving the area of the original Bedford estates and entering what was once a 9-acre field known as Cantelowes Close, owned by the Dukes of Newcastle. It stretched from Bedford Square to what is now Chenies Street, and was bought by the Bedfords from the Newcastles in 1777. The field was rapidly built over, but of the original houses only one (**No.43**) survives. Mary Wollstonecraft (1759-97) was living

in Store Street when she wrote her *Vindication of the Rights of Women* in 1791.

Store Street also saw the birth of the first Dillon's bookshop, opened here by Una Dillon in 1937. The south side of the street has been redeveloped in recent times in imitation Georgian manner, while the north side is dominated by the strong façade of the College of Law (ca.1960). **No.16** Store Street was once a music-hall.

As we continue west, the ground beneath us changes again. On the east side of Tottenham Court Road, and embracing what is now Alfred Place and North and South Crescents, once lay a small estate belonging to the Corporation of the City of London, the revenues of which (they cannot have been great) were devoted to the education of poor City boys. Appropriately, the west side of Alfred Place today houses the City of London Education Department's London Central Careers Unit. Unlike Cantelowes Close, this small estate was never acquired by the Bedfords but was developed by the City itself. Laid out in the early years of the 19th century, it was apparently intended to be something of a prestige development, hence the unexpected width of Alfred Place, to allow uninterrupted views of the crescents at either end. The houses were designed by the Corporation surveyor George Dance the Younger (1741-1825), living at nearby 91 Gower Street, and were allegedly modelled on a proposed

improvement to the Port of London. None, however, have survived.

SOUTH CRESCENT offers us pleasant surprises. On our left as we face it is the Building Centre, originally built just after WW I by the Daimler company as their London showroom in a strikingly handsome classical composition, with a concave front to the Crescent. Next, in the centre, is a harmonious, unpretentious Edwardian building attractively festooned with ivy, originally another school but now **Imagination House**, the home of a design and communications consultancy. Completely remodelled internally and with a flying fabric canopy connecting the Store Street frontage with another 5-storey block to the rear, the building won the Royal Fine Arts Commission/Sunday Times 'building of the year' award in 1989. None of these splendours is visible from the street, though the canopy can be glimpsed from Bedford Square or Gower Mews. To the right of Imagination House a simple classical building, now housing various personal computer companies, completes the composition.

Turning our backs on South Crescent, we proceed up **ALFRED PLACE**. On our right, **No.31**, now Remax House (UCL Economics Department), was once a Jewish girls' club, destroyed with considerable loss of life in April 1941 together with the West Central synagogue next door. Beyond it comes the modern granite and glass structure of Whittington

House, home to HNB Furniture Systems Ltd and various industrial tribunals. To the left, buildings surviving from c.1860 continue round the corner into **CHENIES STREET**.

Our eyes are first drawn to the curious structure which blocks our view of North Crescent. Looking rather like an unfinished Underground station, it is the Chenies Street entrance to the Goodge Street warren of underground tunnels built in 1941/2 as one of eight purpose-built deep shelters in London. These shelters were not intended for the general public, and most ended up as communications centres. The Goodge Street complex was made available to General Eisenhower (hence its name, 'The Eisenhower Centre') at the end of 1942, becoming the signals centre for the Supreme HQ, Allied Expeditionary Force (SHAEF). Much of the planning for D-Day was done here. The Chenies Street entrance was extended after the war when the shelter was adapted for use as an army transit station. In May 1956 a serious fire broke out, and the shelter ceased to be used for accommodation, becoming eventually a security archive. In front is a memorial to the fallen of the 12th County of London Regiment, which seems to have been involved in more than its share of military disasters (Crete, Gazala, Bir Hacheim).

Glancing briefly into **NORTH CRESCENT** itself we can pause to admire the florid baroque of Minerva House (again, once a garage and car showroom), enlivened by touches of art deco and complete with a life-size statue of Minerva herself.

The north side of Chenies Street consists of early 20th-century apartment blocks. 100 years earlier, Fanny Burney (1752-1840), author of *Evelina*, moved in with her sister at No.23 for her last decades. The handsome frontage of the RADA building on the south side is worth a glance, as is the extraordinary 'medieval' tower, complete with crenellations, which rises to the west of it. At the foot of the tower is the **Drill Hall**, built as such in the 1880s for 'Saturday-night soldiers' but reopened as a 'mixed-arts' centre by the Mayor of Camden in November 1976.

Off Chenies Street lies the southern stretch of **HUNTLEY STREET**. A canyon of 19th-century flats, those on the east side are in fact the backs of Nos.12-89 Ridgmount Gardens. Those on the west side, despite their high-sounding names, are particularly ugly and mean-spirited. In 1978, when the Regional Health Authority was planning, amid considerable local opposition, to turn them into flats for UCH staff, they became the scene of a massive squat from which the squatters could be evicted only after Camden Council had agreed to rehouse them. Several of the leaders faced criminal charges, but were acquitted on the grounds that although the flats had been turned into fortresses no actual violence was offered.

On the corner where Huntley Street crosses Torrington Place stands the **Marlborough Arms**, part of a block of altogether more successful turn-of-the-century buildings. Turn right and right again into **RIDGMOUNT GARDENS**. Originally known as Chenies Mews, this was developed in the late 18th century. When the leases fell in in the 1880s the whole street was comprehensively redeveloped into flats for "other than the artisan or labouring classes". The result is quite pleasing, though the narrow strip of garden is awkward of access and must be of aesthetic rather than recreational value.

With a glance into **RIDGMOUNT STREET** (smart modern maisonettes to the left, offices to the right) we can now turn back into Chenies Street and hence to Goodge Street station.

Route 2C.1
Around Bedford Square

From Tottenham Court Road Underground station, take the exit *Tottenham Court Road, East*, walk northwards past the Dominion Theatre (p 36), and turn right into **GREAT RUSSELL STREET**, originally built around 1670 along the line of an old field path, marked as the Green Lane on maps before 1600. By 1720 the street was lined with handsome private residences, including one built for himself by Christopher Wren (1632-1723). This mansion was demolished about 1820 and replaced by four houses. After the palatial houses on the north side, with their great gardens and park with open views to Hampstead and Highgate, had disappeared there was steady decline, with the south side degenerating into commercial properties throughout the 19th century.

First on the right, at the corner with Tottenham Court Road, the Barbados tourist showroom (with Commission above) was opened in March 1986. On the north you see the London Central YMCA building (Elsworth Sykes Partnership), opened in 1976, more harmonious than most buildings of that decade. Its predecessor, an Edwardian baroque building (R Plumbe, Fig 19), opened by Royalty in 1912 as the YMCA flagship, catered to members of HM Forces during WW I. It was hit by a bomb in September 1940 but was quickly repaired, with

---

Street names along route 2C.1 and their origin

Adeline
Wife of 10th Duke of Bedford
Bayley
Sir John Bayley, a celebrated Victorian judge, lived at 41 Bedford Square in the 1820s
Bedford
Ubiquitous name on the estate of the dukes of Bedford
Bloomsbury
Corruption of Blemundsbury
Morwell
One of the estates given to John Russell by Henry VIII
Russell
Family name of the dukes of Bedford

Government help, to serve the same function during WW II. Women were admitted into membership in 1960 and in 1971 the building was completely rebuilt to accommodate these new members as well as to provide further facilities, including the St Giles Hotel on the upper floors, which was at first run as part of the YMCA but became independent around 1990.

This stretch of the street, as far as the traffic lights at Bloomsbury Street, once consisted of modest 18th-century houses of which only one remains: **No.14**, the last house before the open car park on the right. It bears a blue plaque inscribed "Here lived Charles Kitterbell, as related by Charles Dickens in *Sketches by Boz*, 'The Bloomsbury Christening'". The houses before that are 19th-century replacements, sadly run down, except for **No.7**, Nederlander House, with attractive art deco frontage.

Past the car park, the demure building by Lutyens, 1930-2, built to house the YWCA headquarters, is now the Central Club Hotel. Then comes the headquarters of the Trades Union Congress, Congress House (David du R Aberdeen), opened 1958, with striking sculpture above the portico by Bernard Meadows symbolising the spirit of trade unionism. Inside, in the courtyard, Epstein's sculpture of a mother carrying a dead son commemorates the sacrifices of trade unionists in two world wars. The whole of the site from here to Tottenham Court Road, including the Dominion Theatre, was once occupied by a huge Meux brewery (p 88).

Just past the TUC, we see the side of Parnell House (p 88). Now look across to the north side of Great Russell Street, staying on the south side to get a better view and retracing your steps as the numbers increase. Nos.98-107 form an

19 *The first Central YMCA building (1912) in Great Russell Street. Replaced 1971.*

interesting group: several (**Nos.98-99** and **106-107**) date originally from the first development of the street in the 17th century, though refaced and much altered in the 18th and particularly the 19th centuries. There is a parish boundary mark (St Giles/St George's) in the wall of No.99. **Nos.100-102**, now the headquarters of the English Speaking Union, are on the site of, and are believed to incorporate parts of, Thanet House (1686), occupied successively by the Earl of Thanet, his son-in-law the Earl of Leicester and, see the bronze plaque on **No.100**, Topham Beauclerk (1739-1780), descendant of Charles II and Nell Gwynn and friend of Dr Johnson. He was reputed to have such a book collection here that "the British Museum's nose was quite out of joint". His wife was the artist Lady Diana Beauclerk (1734-1808). **No.105-6**, now housing the André Deutsch publishing house, bears a bronze plaque on the upper floors commemorating the architects Augustus Charles Pugin (1702-1832) and his more famous son Augustus Welby Northmore Pugin (1812-1862), who both lived here.

ADELINE PLACE was a feeder road leading from Great Russell Street to Bedford Square. No 18th-century houses remain, the short street being flanked by the YMCA/St Giles Hotel building on the west and mansion flats on the right. Resisting for the moment the temptation to continue into lovely Bedford Square, turn left into the western portion of Bedford Avenue, noting the 1891 Bedford Court Mansions on the corner, and then immediately right into **MORWELL STREET**, whose narrowness reveals that it was formerly a mews for the houses on the western side of Bedford Square, the small houses on the right of the street being the successors to the carriage houses. On the left, the offices of *Time Out* shelter beneath a huge concrete and glass canopy. Note the smart modern hostel of the Alliance Française. Before us, occupying the north-west side of **BAYLEY STREET**, into which we now turn, is the dramatic bulk of the Bedford Corner Hotel (p 37). To the right of the hotel are some 18th-century houses continuing the line of Bedford Square.

BEDFORD SQUARE, 1775-1783, was the first example in London of a square with houses of uniform proportions and design. It seems unscathed by the passage of two turbulent centuries, and is the great survivor of the Golden Age of domestic architecture in London. There are four sides of palace-fronted terraced houses with stucco-faced pedimented centres, surrounding a leafy circular private garden. It combines exterior restraint, even austerity, with the internal magnificence characteristic of the 1770s, when Robert Adam's influence was at its height.

After the Peace of Paris in 1763, which marked Britain's triumph over France in the Seven Years' War, great riches flowed into the country, which according to the 4th Duke of Bedford "excited a rage for building, and houses rose like exhalations". The duke was a great admirer of the King's Circus at Bath, and envisaged a Bedford

Circus on his land in Bloomsbury. After his death in 1771 such a Circus was built on his land in Exeter as two opposing crescents; in London, the idea metamorphosed into a square, developed by his widow, Gertrude Leveson-Gower.

Go round the Square clockwise, enjoying its rich architectural details. The north and south sides each have a central pair of houses surmounted by a pediment; the east and west have a similar pediment but over a single large house. There are several shoe-scrapers surviving from the days when the approach from the north was across muddy fields. The broad paving in front of the north and south sides was added only in the 1980s.

The architect Thomas Leverton designed Bedford Square as a whole, although houses were different inside. They are of plain London stock brick, with deep stone or stuccoed first-floor string courses, stone cornices and dormered mansards. Most striking are the rusticated doorcases made of the artificial 'Coade stone', a sort of glazed terracotta, first made in Lambeth in 1769. The secret of its manufacture was lost for many years, but has now been rediscovered through analysis by the British Museum Research Laboratory.

The first leases for the houses had to be signed by two duchesses (Bedford and Marlborough) and by Robert Palmer (the 4th duke's man of business), and the lessee was precluded from doing anything in or

upon the premises which "may be or grow to the annoyance, grievance, damage or disturbance of the said duchesses and Robert Palmer *or their heirs*". This last condition governs the behaviour of lessees (including the University of London) to this day throughout the Bedford estate.

From the start, the evident intention was that the district should be high-toned and orderly. The quality requirements laid on the builders were stringent: facings, balustrades and windowsills had to be of Portland stone, roofs of slate, gutters and rainwater pipes of lead, floors of best Memel or Riga wood, the pavements wide and of York stone. Coach houses and stables were provided on three sides of the square, in what are now Gower Mews (p 65), Morwell Street (p 69) and Bedford Avenue (p 72).

In the late 18th century the prime development areas for the upper middle classes were Marylebone and Bloomsbury. Bedford Square attracted residents who, though stylish, were not in the Mayfair class nor even quite up to Portland Place. Whereas Berkeley Square in 1792 boasted 16 members of the aristocracy, including two duchesses, Bedford Square had just two lords. It was the aristocracy of the Inns of Court and to some extent of the City who flocked to Bedford Square. It remained a safe residential haven until 1890 and only gradually declined into offices and institutions (including publishers and learned societies) over the next 50 years. The gates across the roads which had protected the Bedford Estate from the riff-raff for over a century (see also p 30) were finally removed in 1890-1893, and Gower Street became, like Tottenham Court Road, a north-south thoroughfare which passed right through Bedford Square past its formerly best side.

The well-known or famous residents of Bedford Square over the years might fill a book on their own. Let us start with the blue plaques: on the west side Thomas Wakley (founder of *The Lancet*) and immediately after him Thomas Hodgkin (another physician, reformer and philanthropist, after whom Hodgkin's disease is named), both at **No.36**. It is perhaps appropriate that the Architectural Association occupies three of the choicest houses in London, **Nos.34-36**. **No.31** was home to Sir Edward Lutyens during WW I and it was there, after the war, that he designed the Cenotaph in Whitehall. On the south lived Sir Anthony Hope-Hawkins (*alias* Anthony Hope, author of *The Prisoner of Zenda*) at **No.41**, William Butterfield (the Gothic-revival architect) at **No.42**. Thomas Leverton himself lived at **No.13** (north side) from 1795 to 1824, as did a later important architect, Lewis Cubitt (p 45) from 1849 to 1867. The Lord Chancellor Lord Eldon (a notorious advocate of hanging for petty offences) occupied **No.6** from 1804 to 1815. This was for long the official residence of Lord Chancellors, and the Square was consequently inhabited over many years by distinguished lawyers and judges, too numerous to mention here.

Representing the arts at one time or another were two knighted actors (Sir Seymour Hicks, also founder of what is now the Gielgud Theatre, at **No.53** and Sir Johnston Forbes-Robertson at **No.22**), three authors (Weedon Grossmith at **No.1** 1902-1919, Anthony Hope at **No.41** 1903-1917 and A J A Symons, biographer of Fr. Rolfe, 'Baron Corvo', at **No.17**), poets Edward Fitzgerald (**No.19**, 1844-8) and Robert Bridges (**No.52**, 1877-1891) and a musician (Sir George Thomas Smart, organist at the coronations of George IV, William IV and Victoria). Even a scientist, the Hon Henry Cavendish (for more details see p 65), is recorded as living at plush **No.11** - which he was able to afford as he inherited a fortune from his aristocratic uncle. **No.51** ought to carry a plaque, but doesn't, to the philanthropist John Passmore Edwards, who lived here but spent his publishing fortune endowing free libraries, hospitals and other public facilities. Former Prime Minister Asquith, after retiring as leader of the Liberals in 1926, moved to Bedford Square for a while, until his wife found the house too small for satisfactory entertaining.

Another significant 'resident' of Bedford Square was the Ladies' College opened at **No.47** (south side) in 1849, which became a School of London University in 1880 and received a Royal Charter as Bedford College for Women in 1909. When the College moved to Regent's Park in 1913, the name was retained, but since its absorption into the Royal Holloway College at Egham, Surrey in the 1980s the name has vanished - although it once again has a Bedford Square office (No.11)!

The best side of Bedford Square was originally the east, as these houses backed on to the gardens of Montague House, the first home of the British Museum, with views all the way to the grounds of Bedford House (Bloomsbury Square, p 80), which were not built over until the early 1800s.

Worth a special look are: beautiful fanlights over several doors, eg **No.7**; **No.6** in the middle of the east side - the largest house in the Square (now the HQ of Barclays Bank); the lamp-holder and link extinguisher outside **No.4**; the narrowness of No.2; and finally the glories of Leverton's **No.1**, including the stuccoed entrance with its curving steps and railings and the 'triumphal arch' containing the door. The picture (p 72) shows a part of its spare, elegant interior.

Next to No.1 to the south is No.60 **BLOOMSBURY STREET**, which now links Bedford Square with Shaftesbury Avenue. The street was called Charlotte Street until 1894. Some of its houses date from the 17th century, though given 18th-century façades. Turn right down it.

Glance to the right as you pass **BEDFORD AVENUE**. This was formerly the lane which ran past the coach-houses for houses on the south side of Bedford Square. In 1891 those on the right were replaced by a uniform row of red-brick coach houses built as a terrace with simple accommodation above, which are now occupied by small businesses. They face the monumental frontage, on the south side, of a block of mansion flats, confusingly named Bedford Court Mansions like those on the northwest corner of Adeline Place, built at the same time (1891).

The two hotels (Sir Thomas Rhind, 1910) flanking Great Russell Street on the west side of Bloomsbury Street were originally called the *Ivanhoe* and the *Kenilworth*, evidently named by a Walter Scott enthusiast, but the Ivanhoe has now become the *Marlborough*, presumably because of the connection with one of the duchesses signing the leases of Bedford Square houses (p 70).

From here you can either take a bus southwards, return to Tottenham Court Road Tube station, or continue along route 2C.2.

20 The entrance hall of No.1 Bedford Square in 1930.

Route 2C.2
Along the greater part of Great Russell Street

This walk begins at the eastern corner of Bloomsbury Street and Great Russell Street, reached either by buses from the north down Gower Street, buses from the west along New Oxford Street or on foot from Tottenham Court Road Underground station. Walk eastwards.

On the left, **No.91**, an original Georgian house with an elegant frieze above the door, bears a blue plaque marking the home (1863-8) of George du Maurier (1834-96), most famous for his novel *Trilby* (1894). His cartoon here entitled "the artist's studio" was accepted for *Punch* a few years before he lived here. On the corner of the first tiny street on the right, **WILLOUGHBY STREET**, there used to be a famous Poetry Bookshop (No.38 Great Russell Street).

On your left you see the British Museum looming, but for the moment concentrate on the modest houses and streets opposite it. These streets were originally developed

21 Punch cartoon (1860) incorporating a self-portrait of George du Maurier, aged about 26 (the artist leading the way into a photographer's studio, Whistler behind him).

PHOTOGRAPHER. "*No Smoking here, Sir!*"

DICK TINTO. "*Oh! A thousand pardons! I was not aware that——*"

PHOTOGRAPHER (interrupting, with dignified severity). "*Please to remember, Gentlemen, that this is not a Common Hartist's Studio!*"——[N.B. Dick and his friends, who are Common Artists, feel shut up by this little aristocratic distinction, which had not yet occurred to them.]

in the 1660s and 1670s on the Earl of Southampton's estate as part of the 'little town' surrounding Southampton Square. After Coptic Street (p 87) Nos.43-48 (notice the gargoyle heads incorporated into the cornice) include **No.46** with a blue

---

Street names along route 2C.2 and their origin

Bury
Abbreviation of Bloomsbury
Galen
Greek physician
Gilbert
Gilbert Holles, Earl of Clare, friend of William Lord Russell
Montague
1st Duke of Montagu married stepsister of Lady Rachel Russell and built Montagu House
Museum
Refers to British Museum
Pied Bull
18th-century inn in Museum Street
Russell
Family name of dukes of Bedford
Willoughby
Mr G P, mayor of Holborn 1904

---

plaque for Randolph Caldecott (1846-86), artist and book illustrator, who first made his name with illustrations for an 1875 edition of Washington Irving's *Sketch Books*.

The inn on the corner of Museum Street is on the site of the *Dog and Duck* hostelry, which may have begun serving alcoholic refreshment informally as early as 1703, when it was an isolated building on the corner of a liquorice field. Duck-hunting, with dogs to retrieve the birds, must have been common on the numerous ponds in the Bloomsbury fields north of here. The pub was renamed the British Museum Tavern in 1762 (the British Museum opened to the public in 1759). It was rebuilt in 1798, extended and refaced in 1855, and remodelled inside in 1889, after its name had been abbreviated (1873) to **Museum Tavern**. The remodelling introduced two stained-glass windows, still to be seen in the food bar, which are rare examples of their kind.

Turn down **MUSEUM STREET** and admire on the right an unbroken range of façades with 'Empire' swags in various pastel shades. Despite appearances, these are actually 18th-century houses which were refaced in 1864 by William Finch Hill, who had refaced the Museum Tavern and several other houses opposite.

On the left, **GILBERT PLACE** was built about 1670 by William Lord Russell on the estate he had just acquired by marriage (p 8). None of the original houses survive. **No.29** on the left carries a sunflower ornament revealing an 1880s construction, and has been given a splendid new door surround with *trompe l'oeil* 'Renaissance' panels. Further along

on this side, one sees only the back of Helen Graham House (p 77). At the opposite end on the right, **Nos.8-10** began life as a 19th-century warehouse.

Return to Museum Street, where in the block between Gilbert Place and Little Russell Street, at first-floor level on **No.40** hangs a bronze sign for George Allen & Unwin. George Allen, a former pupil of Ruskin's, was his publisher. Ruskin is said to have designed the sign, but if so it must have been for Allen alone since Ruskin died before Allen merged with Unwin and moved here. Notice on the south-west corner of Museum Street and Little Russell Street the carved brick cartouches on an otherwise plain late Victorian red brick building; also the Plough, a relatively unspoilt pub of some antiquity.

Now turn left into **LITTLE RUSSELL STREET**. No.21 is one of several small houses from the early 1700s that were refaced in the 19th century. One of them was once the home of the poet W H Davies (1871-1940). The grimy exterior of the back of St George's Bloomsbury on the right belies the beauties within. Go through the narrow passageway, with steps, to the west of the church, emerging into **BLOOMSBURY WAY**; or if the passageway is blocked off, backtrack into Museum Street and reach Bloomsbury Way that way. This was, we believe, the site of the western end of Blemund's Ditch, dug in the 13th century to drain the swamp and which ran from east to west, parallel to the Green Lane. Squint upwards at the extraordinary stepped spire modelled on Pliny's description of the ancient Mausoleum at Halicarnassus, surmounted by a statue of George I (Fig 22). Wren had at one time toyed with the idea of such a spire for St Paul's, and his one-time assistant Hawksmoor is thought to have been inspired thereby to construct this interesting monstrosity.

Now enter the church by the broad steps and six-columned portico in front. **St George's Bloomsbury**, 1716-1731, is one of fifty new churches (only twelve were built) ordained by the Act of 1711 to remedy the shortage of churches in London and Westminster and their growing suburbs. The new parish, detached from St Giles, was to serve the newly fashionable area created in the wake of the construction of Southampton, Montagu and Thanet Houses. The church was constructed on a cramped site purchased from Lady Rachel Russell and already hemmed in by houses. It was a triumph for Hawksmoor that he was able to create a magnificent interior orientated

22 'Prospect' of St George's, Bloomsbury, showing the lion and the unicorn from the royal arms forming 'supporters' to the spire inspired by the Mausoleum at Halicarnassus, with a statue of George I as the pinnacle.

to the east despite the land's north-south axis. However, this design meant that only 447 worshippers could be seated, and an extra 337 seats could be added in 1781 only by adopting a north-south orientation, as originally proposed by Vanbrugh, and inserting galleries. The ingeniously designed eastern apse whereby Hawksmoor achieved the desired orientation can still be seen, with its ceiling decoration intact. The massive white columns with gilt Corinthian capitals give this small church great distinction. The funeral of Emily Davison, the suffragette who died after flinging herself at the king's horse in the Derby in 1913, was held here.

On leaving the church turn left, pursuing Bloomsbury Way (known until the 1930s as Hart Street) between commercial and government buildings as far as **BURY PLACE**, originally a narrow track from High Holborn to Bloomsbury Fields. In about 1662 it was widened to take farm produce and traffic to the new Bloomsbury Market at Barter Street (p 83). Across Bloomsbury Way, on the southeast corner of Bury Place, is an indecisive piece of modern architecture housing the headquarters of BUPA.

Turn left into Bury Place, past the inevitably named Russell Chambers, and then right into a pedestrianised courtyard, **GALEN PLACE**, which continues the line of Little Russell Street. This was named after the 2nd-century Greek physician when it contained the examination halls of the Pharmaceutical Society nearby in Bloomsbury Square (p 80). Galen Place was tidied up in the 1980s after the planning blight (p 39) ended, and now contains at **No.12** the Bloomsbury Workshop, which sells books and other artefacts by members of the Bloomsbury Group (p 13).

A passageway beside the wine bar leads past a covered passage, which now provides access to Bloomsbury Square, into **PIED BULL YARD**, another cleaned-up product of the 1980s in which cheerful white tables for open-air eating and drinking have replaced the farm carts from former times, and smart graphic designers and specialty camera shops have replaced the stables which later became lockup garages.

An archway leads back into Bury Place, where we turn right under an interesting clock to return to Great Russell Street. On the north-east corner, **No.66** Great Russell Street was the first London office of Thomas Cook, which offered board and lodging to visitors. Revamped, together with **No.22 Bury Place**, in 1978, it became the Clover Press, publishing house and retail bookseller. **Nos.66-71**, originally designed by a 25-year-old John Nash, retain their clean Georgian lines.

Across the road, on the corner of Montague Street, **No.77** (with a pretty balcony) bears a blue plaque to the architect Thomas Henry Wyatt 1807-1880, who lived and died here. The Bedford Estate office is at 29a **MONTAGUE STREET**, a street built by Burton and his contemporaries in a nicely uniform style. It leads past the British Museum to Russell Square (p 55). Arthur Conan Doyle lodged at **No.23** when first in London, and his *The Sign of Four* has Sherlock Holmes living in Montague Street.

Now turn back along our last stretch of **GREAT RUSSELL STREET**. First in historical importance on the south side was No.62 (now replaced by Museum Mansions, Nos.62-64) where the **Bloomsbury Dispensary** was founded in 1801. This served the health needs of the poor inhabitants both of the slums of St Giles to the south and those of Little Coram Street and its neighbours to the north. Edward Jenner (p 56) delivered free smallpox vaccination here and served on the Dispensary's medical committee from its inception until his death in 1823. The Dispensary also had the distinction of appointing London's first Medical Officer of Health, in 1846. Bombed in May 1941, it moved into temporary premises that July and in 1942 to 22 Bloomsbury Street (p 88). The introduction in 1948 of the National Health Service made the Dispensary redundant, but it continues to this day as a charity, making grants for preventive health care and holiday relief for carers of the disabled.

In 1827, the American ornithologist and bird artist Audubon (1785-1851) took lodgings at No.55, while looking for an engraver and wealthy subscribers. **Nos.52-57** now form Helen Graham House (1888-1895), a YWCA hostel.

From here you have a good view of the most famous institution in this book: the **British Museum**. The land here was originally leased by Lady Rachel Russell to the Duke of Montagu, husband of her stepsister, and he had Montagu House built here in 1678, designed by the brilliant scientist/architect Robert Hooke and decorated by Verrio. It was burnt down only 8 years later and rebuilt even more lavishly in fashionable French style, the architect being Pierre Puget.

When an Act of Parliament in 1753 brought together Sir Hans Sloane's antiquities with the manuscript collections of the Cotton family and of Robert Harley, Earl of Oxford, they were assembled in Montagu House, purchased for the purpose by the Crown after the death of the 2nd duke. The antiquities were at first grudgingly shown, by appointment only, to parties of not more than ten people. In 1757 George II gave to the museum the Royal Library of 12,000 volumes and with it the privilege of copyright deposit. Over the next 60 years there arrived Sir William Hamilton's first collection of Greek vases (1772), the Rosetta Stone (1802), the Townley collection of Greek sculpture including the *Discobolos* (1805), the Elgin marbles (1816), the head of Rameses II (1819) and George III's library, presented by George IV in 1823.

Sir Robert Smirke was commissioned to expand the space available, and designed a great quadrangle in a style modelled on several Ionian Greek temples, beginning in 1823. What one sees from the street is the south front which, after the construction of the east and west wings, gradually replaced Montagu House, the last element being demolished in 1845. The drawing (Fig 23) shows visitors about 1840 mounting the great staircase of Montagu House to be greeted, rather startlingly, by some giraffes rather than a duke or duchess.

Smirke's mighty portico rests on a 6-foot concrete base, the first use of concrete for such a purpose in England. Construction of the Museum lasted until well into the 1850s; after Smirke's retirement in 1846 the work passed to his brother Sydney Smirke, who also designed the fine railings in front, and then to the latter's son, Sydney Smirke Jr. Foot-high bronze lions used to mark the Museum boundary, some of which now surround the Duke of Wellington's monument in St Paul's. The plane trees lining the street in front of the museum soften the effect, and are held in great affection by readers.

The sculpture in the central pediment is by Sir Richard Westmacott and is supposed by his own account to represent *The Progress of Civilisation*: starting with primitive Man in the west, the various figures represent the Arts - Astronomy in the centre, Mathematics, Drama, Poetry and Music - and Natural History in the east.

The famous round Reading Room, whose dome can be glimpsed from the street at some points, was not part of the original design but was constructed within Smirke's original quadrangle at the instigation of the Principal Librarian of the time, Sir Anthony Panizzi. In 1852, desperate at the congestion resulting from the ever-expanding collection of books and manuscripts, Panizzi took up the idea (already several times put forward) of constructing a circular building within the square courtyard, but this time coupled it with the newly popular use of cast iron for light and airy buildings. By 1854, after one rejected design, Sydney Smirke produced an acceptable solution incorporating the giant dome (much higher than Panizzi's proposal) which is now internationally famous. Its diameter (140 ft) exceeds that of St Peter's in Rome and is surpassed only by that of the Pantheon in Paris. It was first opened to the public in May 1857.

After World War II, with the book collection again exceeding all bounds, there were plans to demolish the little streets between the British Museum and St George's, Bloomsbury and to build a new, separate British Library with grand, wide spaces between. Vehement opposition to these plans caused the whole area to suffer planning blight for some decades, but when Camden Council found a site for the new Library next to St Pancras railway station the houses hereabouts began to be re-occupied and sensitively restored.

For the north entrance of the British Museum, see Montague Place (p 56).

When the British Library moves into the new building, the book-stacks surrounding the Reading Room will go and the British Museum will be transformed into London's first covered public square. A new multi-level elliptical building will be constructed around the Reading Room, housing exhibition galleries, bookshops and restaurant space. It is due to be opened late in the year 2000. We shall see.

If you are not too tired by the walk, go into the British Museum and enjoy the current exhibitions, or return to Tottenham Court Road for your public transport home.

23   Visitors to the British Museum mounting the Grand Staircase of Montagu House shortly before its demolition.

78

Route 2C.3
Around London's oldest Square

Although Bloomsbury Square can be approached from the west along Great Russell Street or Bloomsbury Way, we start this description from Holborn Underground station on the Central and Piccadilly Lines.

Turn right out of the station and cross diagonally to the south-west corner of **SOUTHAMPTON ROW**. This street, originally Upper King Street, marks the eastern boundary of the Earl of Southampton's estate which subsequently became the Bedford estate. A major thoroughfare since the opening of Kingsway in 1905, most of the buildings on it date from the redevelopment. The Central School of Design (1908, by Lethaby) on the eastern side is worth a rapid glance.

The busy street is lined with large commercial buildings of no great distinction. Cross Vernon Place and continue up the left side of Southampton Row, past massive Victoria House (p 82), as far as Bloomsbury Place. Music-lovers may want to continue a few more yards to the corner of Cosmo Place on the right, to see the blue plaque recording the birth of

the conductor Sir John Barbirolli (1899-1970) at what was then the western edge of an Italian quarter of London. A few houses short of Cosmo Place, at 19 Southampton Row as it was then, lived and worked from 1824 to 1872 Thomas Morson (Fig 24), the first quantitative pharmaceutical chemist in England, co-founder of the Pharmaceutical Society whose first headquarters we shall soon encounter in Bloomsbury Square (p 82).

Street names along route 2C.3 and their origin

Barter
Modern name to recall the presence of Bloomsbury Market
Bloomsbury
Corruption of 'Blemundsbury'
Sicilian
Marble from Sicily was used to pave the Avenue
Southampton
1st Earl of Southampton, Henry VIII's Chancellor, was given Blemundsbury after the Dissolution
Vernon
Elizabeth Vernon was mistress, later wife, of 1st Earl of Southampton

---

Turn into **BLOOMSBURY PLACE**, with pleasant 19th-century houses, although the street is much older, being

part of the original Great Russell Street (Green Lane). A blue plaque on **No.3** records the fact that the physician Sir Hans Sloane (1660-1753) lived here 1695-1742 in a mansion housing his collection of antiquities and curiosities, which eventually became the core of the British Museum. This short street leads into

24 Thomas Morson, England's first scientific pharmacist, owner of dispensing premises at 19 Southampton Row.

BLOOMSBURY SQUARE, originally laid out as **Southampton Square** by the 4th Earl of Southampton in 1660 (see p 9). It is said to be modelled on Covent Garden's 'piazza', but differs from it in that the dominant feature was not a church but the nobleman's mansion and forecourt occupying the whole of the north side (Fig 25). The square was not named as such at first; the three rows of houses were named Allington Row (west), Vernon Row (south) and Seymour Row (east), names derived from the earl's family or connections.

The Square was not developed as an architectural whole. Houses of various sizes were built on the plots, and demolished and replaced at various times, with the result that not a single original house remains. Southampton House (renamed Bedford House in 1754) itself was demolished in 1800 by order of the 5th Duke of Bedford, who retired to the country and commissioned James Burton to build on the estate. Burton's houses here survive as offices, some with typical shallow Regency roofed balconies. Continue round the Square anticlockwise.

Bloomsbury Square gardens on your left were originally laid out by Repton, one of the first town squares to have 'picturesque' (as opposed to geometrical) planting. Under them now is a car park, approached from the east side of the Square. In the middle of the north side of the gardens, the seated statue erected

in 1816 is of the Whig politician Charles James Fox (1749-1806). It shows him dressed as a Roman senator, but anachronistically clutching the Magna Carta. He gazes up Bedford Place (p 56) to the statue of the 5th Duke of Bedford in Russell Square.

No.20 (east of Bedford Place), the house Gertrude Stein lived in briefly in 1902 before moving on to Paris, formerly housed the Paul Mellon Centre for Studies in British Art, now at 16 Bedford Square. **No.17**, the elegant house with frontages on both Great Russell Street and Bloomsbury Square, was originally built in the 17th century but was remodelled into two houses by Nash in 1777/8, one of them for his own occupancy. The two were reconnected and refaced in 1860 by the [now Royal] Pharmaceutical Society of Great Britain, which also added the top floor. The Society moved out in 1976, leaving its former name high up on the Great Russell Street side. The Society built out at the back, into the stable yard which is now Pied Bull Yard (p 76), from which it was but a step to its examination hall in Galen Place (p 76). Nowadays, both little enclaves are reached by a passageway made between Nos.15 and 14 Bloomsbury Square as recently as the 1980s.

In 1981 the whole north-western block, which had been purchased in the expectation of building a new British Library on the site, was sold again for

redevelopment, after lying derelict for years. **Nos.9-13** form an Italianate terrace refaced in the 19th century. **No.9** bears a blue plaque for the dermatologist Dr Robert Willan (1787-1812). **Nos.7-8** date from 1881, in contrast to **Nos.5-6** at the southwest corner, a fine 18th-century building, Charlton House, possibly by Flitcroft (p 82). **No.6** has an ornate carved plaque to "Isaac d'Israeli, Author" 1766-1843, better known to us as the father of Prime Minister Benjamin Disraeli.

On the south side, Nos.1-4 are in a variety of styles and commercial occupation; **Nos.2-3** (now a Coopers & Lybrand Training Centre), was remodelled (1882) for the College of Preceptors, a body formed in 1846 to improve the standard of independent teachers. The south side then continues with Nos.47-46 (confusingly) before we reach the southern exit from the Square, Southampton Place.

Pause on the corner to admire **Nos.1-8 Southampton Place**, which together with **No.45** Bloomsbury Square form a harmonious 18th-century whole. On No.45 is a bronze plaque recording the fact that Philip [Stanhope], 2nd Earl of Chesterfield (1633- 1713), lived here, as did Philip the 3rd earl and Philip the 4th earl (1694-1773). The 4th earl wrote

25 Southampton House and its Square in the early 18th century. Note the uniformity of the houses at this stage.

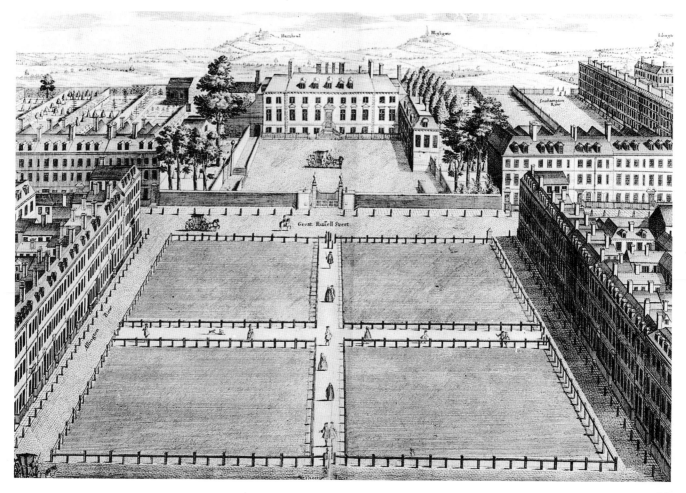

Hamstead   Highgate   Ilington

Southampton Row

Great Ruſſell Street

Allington Row

81

some celebrated letters to his son on how a gentleman should behave. It was he who, when he belatedly offered patronage to Dr Johnson on publication of the great Dictionary in 1752, suffered a famous put-down:

Dr Johnson to the Earl of Chesterfield

The notice which you have been pleased to take of my labours, had it been early, had been kind: but it has been delayed till I am indifferent, and cannot enjoy it: till I am solitary, and cannot impart it: till I am known, and do not want it.

Amongst other famous residents of Bloomsbury Square were two royal physicians: Dr John Radcliffe (1650-1714), physician to William and Mary and benefactor of Oxford University and St Bartholomew's Hospital, and Dr Mark Akenside (1721-1770), a physician to Queen Charlotte (George III's queen) and a poet (see box). Finally, the essayist Richard Steele (1672-1729) lived in Bloomsbury Square 1711-1714 when it was the height of fashion, writing (together with Addison) pungent social satires based on his fashionable acquaintance.

Dr Johnson, of Mark Akenside's poems

One bad Ode may be suffered, but a number of them together makes a man sick.

The Square then continues, with decreasing house numbers, to merge into Vernon Place. Look across at the colossal but harmonious building which occupies the whole of the east side of the Square and the whole block across to Southampton Row. By Charles William Long, Victoria House was purpose-built for the Liverpool Victoria Friendly Society and completed in 1934. The reliefs in the pediment facing the Square represent the bounties of nature, while those facing Southampton Row (not easy to see, even from across that road!) represent industry and navigation, perhaps a reference to Liverpool.

Buried under Victoria House are the foundations of Lord Mansfield's house at Nos.28-9 Bloomsbury Square, which was sacked and burned during the Gordon Riots; he and his wife barely escaped with their lives out of the back door on to Southampton Row. The architect Edwin Lutyens had his office (and lived) at No.29 from 1897 to 1910, a highly important period for him, when he received commissions (amongst many others) to design Hampstead Garden Suburb and New Delhi.

The traffic-bound **VERNON PLACE** continues the line of Bloomsbury Way. It was named after Elizabeth Vernon, mistress and belatedly wife of the Earl of Southampton to whom Henry VIII had given the manor of Blemundsbury. The north side is occupied entirely by

26 *Cast-iron baluster within No.5 Bloomsbury Square (Charlton House).*

the side of Victoria House, the south by commercial buildings, built as a piece with charming **SICILIAN AVENUE** in 1905. This pedestrian precinct, cutting diagonally across the SW corner of Vernon Place with Southampton Row, is screened at each end by a row of Corinthian columns in yellow terracotta. Well known for its bookshops and cafés, the avenue is said to be paved with Sicilian limestone.

Retrace your steps to **SOUTHAMPTON PLACE**, which links Bloomsbury Square and High Holborn. We have already admired Nos.1-8 (p 80); now look at **Nos.14-18** across the way, also very pleasing mid-18th-century, tastefully restored. It is evident, however, that **No.19** was built in the 19th century - right over narrow Barter Street which used to lead to Bloomsbury Market, by that time long discontinued. Go through the tunnel into **BARTER STREET** (originally Silver Street), with some pretty 19th-century shop fronts at this end (Fig 27). At the far end there is a modern office block on an island site. In the 17th and 18th centuries the fish market was here and east of it a meat market (Fig 28). This market area formed part of the Earl of Southampton's original plans for Bloomsbury Square. It supplied food to the residents from the 1660s until 1799, though by then much shrunken in size and profit; there is mention of it as late as 1822. Barter Street makes a right-angled turn to the north; on

27 Barter Street in 1970. Watercolour by Anthony Dracup.

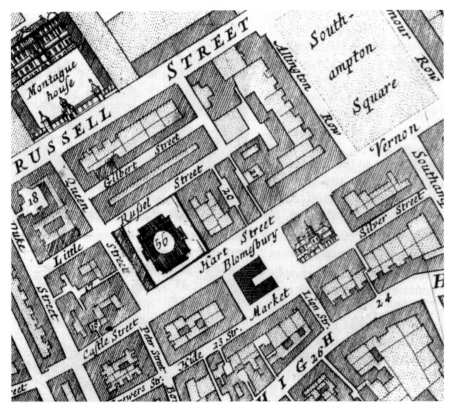

the right are Swedenborg Hall and House, the latter an outlet for literature by and about the 18th-century scientist, mystic and theologian.

Backtrack to Southampton Place, where a bronze plaque on **No.17** states "Here lived Cardinal Newman (1801-1890) in early life", at which time he was Protestant. After his conversion in later life to Catholicism he was one of the pillars of the Catholic church.

A short walk south brings us to High Holborn and thence (left) to our starting point at Holborn Underground station.

28 Bloomsbury Market on a map of 1720. Southampton Square is now Bloomsbury Square, Hart Street is now Bloomsbury Way and Silver Street, Barter Street.

3 Along New Oxford Street

Early in Victoria's reign traffic congestion was becoming a problem in St Giles High Street and in 1840 a Bill was passed to permit the construction of a bypass road running directly from Oxford Street to High Holborn (Fig 29). No fewer than 259 freeholds in the infamous slums known as the St Giles Rookeries were compulsorily purchased, and construction began in 1844. Hundreds of destitute people were left homeless; the Duke of Bedford, as owner of 104 of these freeholds, received £114,000 in compensation.

We shall walk **NEW OXFORD STREET** from its eastern end, where it forks off from High Holborn before the latter makes its southward swoop to St Giles High Street. This unusual feature for a Roman road - it was part of Watling Street, leading to the crossroads at Marble Arch and then turning north to Edgware - is thought to be due to the originally extremely swampy nature of the ground. Here we are cutting across the south-eastern tip of the old manor of Blemundsbury, which from about 1605, under a dispensation of James I, who was well-disposed to the dashing 3rd Earl of Southampton, extended southwards from

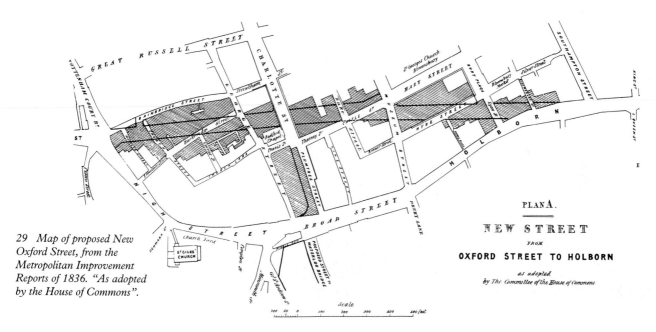

29 Map of proposed New Oxford Street, from the Metropolitan Improvement Reports of 1836. "As adopted by the House of Commons".

the manorhouse a short distance north of here all the way to High Holborn and Broad Street, St Giles. Blemund's Dyke or Ditch, which was dug to drain at least part of the swamp, lay - if we make a rough judgement from the not always accurate early maps - along the line of Vernon Place, just north of the manorhouse, as far as the western end of present Bloomsbury Way.

We shall use the modern numbering of New Oxford Street, which starts from the east end, with odd numbers on the south and even numbers on the north of the Street. (Originally, Oxford Street numbers were continued into the new 'extension', with continuous numbering from 441 on the south side, returning on the north side to end in 550.) You can reach our starting point from Holborn Underground station by crossing Kingsway and following High Holborn for a short stretch, then forking right. Apart from buses, there is only a trickle of westbound traffic here, between a row of small shops on the south side (**Nos.1-19**) surmounted by dull buildings, and St George's Court on the north, an equally dull Government building. It must have been much busier in the early 20th century, with parties of weary parents and their offspring crossing from Hamley's toyshop, then a bit further west at No.35, to the Express Dairy Tea Rooms where St George's Court is now. Another place of refreshment here, the popular Vienna

restaurant on the corner with Bloomsbury Way (Nos.24-28), was demolished in 1939.

New Oxford Street was completed by 1847 and the vacant sites were soon taken up by such buildings as **Nos.33-37**, about

30   Changing books in Mudie's subscription library, 1901.

1850, with shops at street level and dwellings above. New Oxford Street quickly became a commercial success, attracting a wide range of shops, offices, banks and warehouses. An early arrival was Charles Mudie, who moved his business from 28 Upper King Street (now Southampton Row) in 1852 to a spacious site (Nos.30-34) on the northwest corner of New Oxford Street with Museum Street (at the fork with Bloomsbury Way), where he built Mudie's Select Library (Fig 30). Mudie's (including branches in Manchester and Birmingham) had as many as 120,000 books in circulation at a time, with a further million books in reserve. Readers could borrow one book at a time for a guinea (£1.05) a year. Early subscribers included Herbert Spencer and Edward Fitzgerald. The original building has been replaced by another, inhabited in 1997 by 'Initiative Media' above and 'Deep Pan Pizza' below.

Small businesses, as today, occupied sites between the great Mudie's and Bloomsbury Street, though none as impressive as James Smith & Sons (No.53), prominent across the street on the south side, sole survivor of the splendid Victorian stores which used to grace this street. This handsome shop appeared here (as No.467) in 1865, initially as a branch of the original 1830s establishment off Regent Street. It sells and repairs umbrellas, walking sticks and whips of

every description. It stands on the triangular island formed by the junction of New Oxford Street with the northern end of Shaftesbury Avenue (which actually splits here into two arms embracing the island). On the floor are a few small blue and white Minton tiles from the 'Commonwealth Dairy' which stood here earlier; and sometimes displayed are three

---

Street names along route 3 and their origin

Bainbridge
17th-century builder, possibly father-in-law to Dyott
Coptic
Named when British Museum acquired some Coptic manuscripts
Dyott
Vestryman of St Giles, recorded in 1676
Oxford
Robert Harley, Earl of Oxford owned land at the western end of Oxford Street
Stedham
Unknown
Streatham
Duke of Bedford is also Baron Howland of Streatham (created 1695)
Willoughby
Mr G P, mayor of Holborn 1904

---

photographs of the flag-bedecked building during the celebrations of Queen Victoria's

1897 jubilee. At the eastern end of the island is a defunct water fountain in red granite erected at that time.

Almost opposite the fountain, on the north side of the street, is **STEDHAM PLACE**, a tiny opening between two shops reminiscent of the courts which used to run between the tall houses in the notorious Rookeries, but in this case brightened by charming flowerboxes all up and down the back of Stedham Chambers in Streatham Street (p 88).

Backtrack slightly to the traffic lights, cross New Oxford Street and continue north into **COPTIC STREET**, formerly Duke Street (the duke being the ubiquitous Duke of Bedford), renamed in 1894 when the British Museum nearby had acquired an important collection of manuscripts from the early Christian (Coptic) churches in Egypt. On the west side remain some Victorian houses with shops at street level; on the east, at the NE corner with Little Russell Street, is (**Nos.30-33**) a building inscribed in brick *The Dairy Supply Co Ltd* high up on both streets. This was designed by R P Wellcock in 1888; the date is confirmed by the sunflower motif typical of that decade. Here was one of the earliest wholesale suppliers of milk in Central London; through the wagon-wide entry in Little Russell Street can be seen the remains of the lifting tackle. It was used later by United Dairies. In 1967 a trend-setting scheme by Enzo Apicella slotted a restaurant (Pizza Express) into the previous fittings, retaining the white tiles and stained glass. The forerunner of many theme restaurants, it is of considerable interest to architectural historians.

Turn left into **STREATHAM STREET**, on both SW and NW corners of which stand Stedham Chambers, the south face of which we glimpsed from New Oxford Street. This was a private development of 1886. The far (western) end of Streatham Street, once Woburn Court, is now pedestrianised. Walk past **WILLOUGHBY STREET**, a side road not always included on maps and named Woburn Street on Goad's 1888 map. Note the helmeted classical head (Menelaos), origin unknown, above the porch of the last Streatham Street house on the left before you reach Bloomsbury Street. Opposite, at No.22 Bloomsbury Street, formerly stood the second home of the Bloomsbury Dispensary (p 76), with its main frontage on Streatham Street.

Cross Bloomsbury Street (at the lights!) and continue along the short remainder of Streatham Street to the building on the corner with Dyott Street (these little narrow streets are all leftovers from the St Giles 'Rookeries' on the grotty side of the Bedford estate, separated from the posh part by Great Russell Street). The building is **Parnell House**, one of the earliest of the model dwellings (see the inscription at second-floor level) for the 'deserving labouring classes' erected all over London as slums were cleared. This one was originally Ashlyn's Buildings, opened 1850 (thus, shortly after the construction of New Oxford Street had displaced families from the Rookeries), designed by Henry Roberts on behalf of the Society for Improving the Conditions of the Working Classes, and is the earliest extant building of the kind. (The first in London, bombed in World War II, was Metropolitan Buildings in St Pancras.) It was later adopted by the Peabody Trust. A plaque in the courtyard (very rarely open to the public) was unveiled in 1987 by Sir Hugh Cubitt (descended from the Cubitt family which built so much in Bloomsbury), then the chairman of the Housing Corporation of the Peabody Trust, to celebrate the 125th anniversary of the Trust (which thus dates from 1862) and the reopening of Parnell House after refurbishment.

All 54 flats are entered and chiefly lit from balconies overlooking an internal courtyard, by which device the architect successfully reduced the window tax which made the first apartment blocks expensive to maintain. Ironically, the window tax was abolished in 1851. Each flat contained a living room, scullery, two bedrooms and a water closet off the scullery - a tremendous improvement in sanitation over previous arrangements in the poorest housing - and was let for 4/- (20p) a week. The rent of basement flats was half this.

Parnell House stands on the corner of **DYOTT STREET**, known as such since 1877 but at various times in its history as Maidenhead Lane, Dyot Street and George Street. The first houses in the street (actually in the southern part, near St Giles church) were built by Henry Bainbridge about 1672; his daughter was Jane Dyot or Dyott, possibly the wife of Simon Dyott, a vestryman of St Giles parish, listed in a survey of 1676. Glance down **BAINBRIDGE STREET**, which today is a gloomy canyon between the backs of buildings on New Oxford Street and Great Russell Street. From 1809 the north side of this street was dominated by Meux's vast Horseshoe Brewery, a greatly enlarged version of the first brewery founded here by Blackburn and Bywell. Sir Henry Meux installed a giant vat there holding 3555 gallons, but this burst its metal hoops in 1814 and the resulting flood of beer destroyed three adjacent houses, with the loss of eight lives. The brewery was finally demolished in 1922 and eventually replaced by the buildings of the TUC and YWCA (p 68).

Turn left down Dyott Street to regain New Oxford Street and turn right. The southward continuation of Dyott Street across the street would take us into the heart of the area known until 1847 as the St Giles Rookeries, the story of which belongs in another book.

The block on the north side of New Oxford Street between Dyott and Bloomsbury Streets, Isis House, is modern and replaces bombed property. On the western corner with Dyott Street, at No.78, were the offices of Thomas Holloway, purveyor of pills and ointments. He founded (Royal) Holloway College at Egham, Surrey, in 1886 for wealthy young women; this became part of London University in 1900 (see also p 71).

Henry Glave, Linen Drapers, were in business at adjacent Nos.80-88 by the 1880s. The firm was described on an 1888 map, like others nearby, as a warehouse - a description that Victorians thought more respectable than 'shop'. Glave's also occupied one of the shops in the short-lived Royal Arcade, "a miniature imitation of the Burlington Arcade" according to Barton, the entrance to which was next to Glave's first shop. In 1929 Gunton & Gunton rebuilt Glave's, which had by this time been extended westwards to include Nos.90-112, in imposing neo-classical style; but within a few years (1936) the firm closed. The handsome building, with giant Corinthian pilasters, can still be admired from across the street above the modern, often tawdry shop fronts.

31 A view of the elaborate interior of the main office of Pears' soap (later, a bank), 71-75 New Oxford Street, about 1900.

Swan and Edgar occupied the building for a time. Now known as Prospect House, it is a listed building and houses part of the MOD.

Look across at the triple bay of **Nos. 71-75**, once the famous offices (W B Catherwood, 1887) of A & F Pears, soap manufacturers, with an elaborate façade of brick and Portland Stone. It once boasted an interior (p 89) "remarkable for its decoration in the Italian style - mosaics, marble statuary, fountains and pools" - and naturally, with an emphasis on bathing and cleanliness. On the upper floor, reached by a marble staircase, were hung paintings the firm paid a great deal of money for, including Millais' *Bubbles*, possibly the first painting by a serious artist ever sold for a commercial purpose. The Midland Bank took over the building in the 1920s, but its former glories have vanished into the maw of *Forbidden Planets* on the ground floor, and the Atlantic Hostel above.

Next door at **Nos.77-91** is the enormous and utterly plain Castlewood House, Government and private offices, stretching well back along Earnshaw Street. The original No.91, now part of Castlewood House, was occupied for the best part of a century - from before 1860 until WW II - by John S Deeds & Sons, curriers and leather factors.

EARNSHAW STREET was named after Thomas Earnshaw, 1749-1829, inventor of the modern chronometer escapement and balance, whose workshop at 119 High Holborn is marked with a plaque.

Before Glave's expanded westwards, at No.108 (in 1997, a Chinese restaurant) stood the chemist's shop (Lewis and Burrows) where Dr Crippen signed the poisons register on 19 January 1910 in buying 5 grains of hyoscine hydrobromide intended for his wife. Crippen, a dentist, was a partner in the Yale Tooth Specialist Co. at Nos.57-61, Oxford Mansions (now glass-fronted Albion House) on a site originally occupied by the Unitarian Bedford Chapel (1771, demolished late 19th century). His mistress Ethel Le Neve worked here too, as a typist and bookkeeper; his wife, as treasurer of the Music Hall Ladies' Guild, attended its weekly committee meetings in Dr Crippen's suite of offices. Crippen and Le Neve were arrested on board ship off Canada on 31 July 1910 as the result of the first police use of wireless communication. Crippen was hanged on 23 November.

The innovative firm of Imhofs (founded 1845) had moved into **Nos.114-116** by 1904. The 1860 directory described Daniel Imhof as a (German) organ builder, but he also invented the orchestrion, a clockwork instrument that played orchestral music. He seems to have been the first shopkeeper to sell a gramophone. His wife Kathleen gave the first gramophone recital at Queen's Hall in 1910. In 1929 the firm rebuilt their headquarters as Imhof House, with the same skyline and white stone facing as Glave's but with less dignity. Moving with the times, Imhofs sold radios, records and television sets, finally closing only in 1981. The tradition is continued in an electronic superstore on the ground floor.

The firm previously at No.103 (a number adjacent to the National Westminster bank at No.101, but demolished by the modern traffic arrangements) was, in 1900, the sole maker and supplier of the Burton Gillette Horse Clipping and Sheep Shearing Equipment.

Finally we come to the corner with Tottenham Court Road, where early in the 20th century Horne Bros, men's outfitters, were set up at **No.118** and where in the 1930s Montague Burton, 'the fifty-shilling tailor' built a grand six-storey shop at a cost of £300,000. 'Burton' is still in business there today.

The extraordinarily out-of-scale building, Centre Point, which looms to the south over this ancient cross-roads was a speculative venture of the 1960s which failed financially and will remain as a monument to 20th-century folly and greed well into the future.

Sources

Bailey, Nick. *Fitzrovia* (Historical Publications, in association with Camden History Society, 1981)

Bebbington, Gillian. *London street names* (Batsford, 1972)

Booth, Charles. *Life and labour of the people in London* (Macmillan, 1892-7). 9 vols and 1 vol of maps

Byrne, Andrew. *Bedford Square: an architectural study* (British Museum Publications, 1990)

Byrne, Andrew. *London's Georgian houses* (Georgian Press, 1986)

Caygill, Marjorie. *The story of the British Museum* (British Museum Publications, 1992)

Chancellor, E Beresford. *London's old Latin Quarter* (Cape, 1930)

Clinch, George. *Bloomsbury and St Giles past and present; with historical and antiquarian notices of the vicinity* (Truslove & Shirley, 1890)

Clinch, George. *Marylebone and St Pancras: their history, celebrities, buildings and institutions* (Truslove & Shirley, 1890)

Clunn, Harold P. *The face of London* (Rev ed. Phoenix House, 1957)

Crook, J Mordaunt. *The British Museum: a case-study in architectural politics* (Allen Lane, 1972)

Davis, Eliza Jeffries. 'The University site, Bloomsbury.' In *London Topographical Record* vol XVII, 1936, pp 19-139

Department of the Environment. *List of buildings of special architectural or historic interest as at 14 May 1974, London Borough of Camden* (DOE, 1974)

Fairfield, S. *The streets of London: a dictionary of the names and their origins* (Macmillan, 1983)

Fiber, Sally. *The Fitzroy: an autobiography of a London tavern* (Temple House, 1995)

Gordon, Edward & Deeson, A F L. *The book of Bloomsbury* (Edward Gordon Arts, 1950)

Hamilton Fairley, Sir Neil. 'The Hospital for Tropical Diseases (UCH), London'. *Univ Coll Hosp Magazine* vol 37, 1952, pp 114-8

Harte, Negley & North, John. *The world of University College, London 1828-1978* (UCL, 1978)

Kelly, Alison. *Mrs Coade's stone* (Upton-on-Severn: Self Publishing Association, 1990)

Lees, Lynn Hollen. *Exiles of Erin: Irish migrants in Victorian London* (Manchester U P, 1979)

McAuliffe, Rona. *The story of Bloomsbury Dispensary* (Trustees of the Bloomsbury Dispensary, 1973)

Meade, Dorothy & Wolff, Tatiana. *Lines on the Underground: an anthology for travellers* (Penguin, 1994)

Meller, Hugh. *St George's, Bloomsbury: an illustrated guide to the church* (St George's Church, 1975)

Merrington, W R. *University College Hospital and its Medical School: a history* (Heinemann, 1976)

Miller, E. *That noble cabinet: a history of the British Museum* (André Deutsch, 1973)

Olsen, D J. *Town planning in London: The 18th and 19th Centuries* (2nd ed. Yale University Press, 1982)

Pevsner, Nikolaus. *London, 1: The cities of London and Westminster* (3rd ed, revised by Bridget Cherry, Penguin, 1973)

Pevsner, Nikolaus. *London, except the Cities of London and Westminster* (Penguin, 1952)

Rasmussen, Steen Eiler. *London, the unique city* (1937; abridged version Pelican, 1960)

Richardson, John. *Covent Garden past* (Historical Publications, 1979)

Simpson, Colin. *The Cleveland Street affair* (Weidenfeld & Nicholson, 1977)

Smith, John Thomas. *A book for a rainy day; or recollections of the events of the years 1766-1833* (3rd ed, Richard Bentley, 1861)

Summerson, John. *Georgian London* (4th ed, Penguin, 1988)

Survey of London, vol.XXI (London County Council, 1949)

Tallis, J. *London Street Views* 1838-40

Tames, Richard. *Bloomsbury past* (Historical Publications, 1993)

Tuke, Margaret A. *A history of Bedford College for Women 1849-1937* (Oxford U P, 1939).

Ulph, Colin. *150 not out: the story of the Paymaster General's Office 1836-1986* (Paymaster General's Office, 1985)

Walford, Edward. *Old and new London* (Cassell, 1872-8)

Weinreb, Ben & Hibbert, Christopher (eds). *The London encyclopaedia* (Macmillan, 1983)

Biographical

Bénézit, E. *Dictionnaire critique et documentaire des peinteurs, sculpteurs, dessinateurs et graveurs de tous les temps et de tous les pays* (10 vols)

Dictionary of National Biography

Hobhouse, Hermione. *Cubitt, master builder* (Macmillan, 1971, reprinted 1995)

Who Was Who

Wilson, Jean Moorcroft. *Virgina Woolf, life and London: a biography of place* (Cecil Woolf, 1987)

Maps

Strype 1720; Rocque 1746; Robert Sawyer 1768; Faden 1785; Horwood 1799; Ordnance Survey West End 1870, 1914

Booth's poverty maps, 1889-98

Goad's insurance maps

Bomb damage maps

Other sources

Camden History Review. , Scala Theatre vol 20 pp24-25; Dr Kitchiner vol 6 pp18-19; Col. Edis vol 7 pp15-16; silver tickets vol 12 pp2-5; Sir Samuel Romilly vol 20 pp5-6; Museum Tavern vol 16 pp5-9; Bloomsbury Market vol 14 pp20-23.

Fitzrovia Neighbourhood News

Journal of the Friends' Historical Society

The Tower 1973-79

Census returns

LCC/GLC street lists

Post Office/Kelly's London directories

Camden Local Studies Library & Archive, Theobalds Road, WC1, including the Heal Collection

Guildhall Library, Aldermanbury, EC2

London Metropolitan Archives (formerly GLRO), Northampton Road, EC1

National Monuments Record, 55 Blandford Street, W1

Westminster Archives, St Ann's Street, SW1

Index